PRAYER AND RENEWAL

The Sister Formation Series

The Mind of the Church in the Formation of Sisters, Proceedings for 1954–1955, ed. Sister Ritamary, c.h.m., 1956.

Spiritual and Intellectual Elements in the Formation of Sisters, Proceedings for 1955–1956, ed. Sister Ritamary, c.h.m., 1957.

Planning for the Formation of Sisters, Proceedings for 1956–1957, ed. Sister Ritamary, c.h.m., 1958.

The Juniorate in Sister Formation, Proceedings for 1957–1958, ed. Sister Ritamary, c.h.m., 1960.

The Religious-Apostolic Formation of Sisters, Elio Gambari, s.m.m., 1964.

Program for Progress, Proceedings for 1965, ed. Sister Mary Hester Valentine, s.s.n.d., 1966.

The Local Superior: Capstone of Formation, Proceedings for 1967, ed. Sister Mary Hester Valentine, s.s.n.d., 1968.

Published by Fordham University Press

PRAYER AND RENEWAL

Proceedings and Communications of Regional Meetings
of the Sister-Formation Conferences
1969

Editor

Sister Mary Hester Valentine, s.s.n.d.
Mount Mary College
Milwaukee, Wisconsin

Foreword

Edwin A. Quain, s.j.
Fordham University

FORDHAM UNIVERSITY PRESS
New York · 1970

© Copyright 1970 Fordham University Press

Library of Congress Catalog Card Number: 58–10465
ISBN 0–8232–0875–3

Printed in the United States of America

Table of Contents

v

Foreword

The proceedings of the Sister-Formation Conferences of 1968–69 stemmed from the workshop held at Woodstock College, Woodstock, Maryland in the summer of 1968. That meeting took as its subject three elements in the renewal program of communities of religious women of the United States: *Prayer, Person and Community,* and *Incorporation into the Congregation.* Subsequent conferences, held throughout the various regions, were devoted to commentary and discussion of these three topics, and the resultant papers are here incorporated into this volume of the now fifteen-year-old SISTER-FORMATION SERIES.

It was commendable that a great deal of the study and comment dealt with the centrally important subject of prayer in the life of the religious. It may be taken as a truism that the essence of the religious life should center on the desire of each individual to achieve such union of mind and will and heart with the will of God, as is possible to her, with her natural endowments and the supernatural grace with which she is blessed. The achievement of that union will act as a leaven for all that the religious may do and be, in the eyes of man and God; the strength, the courage, the endurance that will come from supernatural help and guidance will enable the all-too-human creature to be faithful to the commitment made in generosity and love, to serve both God and fellow man in the community to which the Holy Spirit has led. If a true and salutary renewal of religious life is to be found, a renewal that will truly make more efficacious the labor and toil of countless religious for the salvation of souls, it must be guided and directed by the Holy Spirit who will speak to the mind and soul in the periods of silent prayer, a prayer of openness to the behest of the Paraclete "who will teach you all things, and bring all things to your mind, whatsoever I have said to you." For if renewal should bring us to something other than what the Spirit of truth tells us, then we should be false to "the testimony He shall give of me."

It is clear that religious are now allowed considerably more freedom concerning time, place, and manner of prayer, and it is perhaps not idle to underline the fact that such freedom places a greater responsibility on the individual lest this vital contact with the supernatural be diminished. Doubtless, this very freedom has had a liberating effect on the spirit and has unloosed vast stores of energy and zeal which might have been impeded, or even choked off, by adherence to mere routine. However, in these times when we have become conscious of the unexpected effects of changes in the ecology of nature, a fruitful subject for prayerful reflection might be the analogous effects on the very nature of the dedication of a religious that have been occasioned by the alteration of what we might call the ecological balance of the religious life. Such effects, always far-reaching and often unforeseeable, make it imperative that vigilance and care be exercised lest informality in prayer cause a weakening of the desire for prayer—cause a habit of carelessness, not only about prayer but about other essential elements of one's way of life and supernatural orientation. Thus, one's greater dedication to others, in pursuit of "community," could conceivably, just by taking up more and more precious time, leave less time for prayer—in fact, less time for God! But, it will be said: "In serving my neighbor, I am serving God. True, indeed; but if a means to the service of God becomes an end in itself (and thereby frustrates other and more fundamental ends), then there is place for some careful and precise discernment of spirits—in a word, prayerful consideration, before God, of our purity of intention, of our basic honesty. Hence, each individual must be alert to the dangers that lie in wait as we exercise our new-found freedom.

Particularly significant, and worthy of further and deeper study, are the implications of the masterly analyses in this volume of the notion of "community" and "commitment" by Fr. Newbold and Fr. Clarke. For, without any doubt, these are the most fundamental of the changes that have come so rapidly in the last several years. While the institution of religious life may, in the past, have been guilty of a pusillanimous hesitancy in making changes clearly reasonable and demanded by the common good, it would be equally reprehensible if fundamental issues were decided and implemented without sufficient consideration of consequences. As an instance, the shift from large, institutional communities of religious at varying stages of formation and apostolic activity to the desired smaller, more home-like groups will have immense financial implications: large pieces of property, buildings, and educational facilities will presumably lie idle and unused and, unless maintained, will deteriorate; smaller communities will inevitably demand duplication of facilities—hence, added costs. Is it reasonable for those whose personal fulfillment demands a smaller living-group to close their eyes to the responsibility that will fall upon those who have the legal and moral obligation for the financial resources of a community? Financial problems have a way of not going away because they are disregarded; rather they seem to have an innate tendency to become more difficult to handle.

Likewise, the feeling has apparently been growing that indicates the undesirability, if not the moral impossibility, of a person's making a life-time commitment to the religious life. Now, it might be a fruitful source of reflection if we consider the possible effect on one of the smaller living-groups, if it becomes clear (as it inevitably will) that the degree of permanency and dedication of some members of the group is considerably less than that of other members. The perception of "community" (whatever it may be) will surely be nourished and developed by nothing so much as by a common, deeply shared purpose and dedication to accomplish some *one* end. A disparity of interest and dedication among members of a small group (and the smaller the group, the greater the effect) can hardly be concealed, and consequently will be a divisive influence, destructive of any true sense of "community."

Hence, considerable thought should be directed toward the implications of steps being contemplated or, in some cases, already taken. In fact, it would seem that there is great need of a virtue that one might think to have been repealed in recent times: the gift of the Holy Spirit known as prudence. It may be illuminating if we read the note on synonyms of prudence, as given in the most recently published dictionary:

SYNONYMS: *prudence, discretion, circumspection.* These nouns are compared as they express caution and wisdom in the conduct of affairs. *Prudence*, the most comprehensive, implies not only caution but the capacity for judging in advance the probable results of one's actions. *Discretion* suggests prudence coupled with self-restraint and sound judgment. *Circumspection* adds to discretion the implication of wariness in one's actions out of consideration for social and moral consequences.

Such admirable qualities, it would seem, would have a very considerable effectiveness in guiding the judgments now being made by religious in the Church of today and, let us never forget it, of tomorrow.

Fordham University Press   EDWIN A. QUAIN, S.J.

Statement of Purpose:
Sister Formation Conference

The Sister Formation Conference exists to serve religious communities of women in their effort to promote, under the Holy Spirit's guidance, the fullest possible development of their members—spiritual, intellectual, social, professional, apostolic.

The Conference understands the term "formation" as a noun descriptive of the process by which the Holy Spirit forms the Christian person for union with God in the service of His Kingdom. The Conference attributes to the sister herself, under the Spirit, the primary responsibility for her own integrated development.

As the community can only assist the sister, the Conference can only assist the community. It respects the diversity of means selected by the congregations, but it assumes a unanimity of goals among religious congregations as groups publicly consecrated in celibate community within the Church to work for the union of all men in Christ. The Conference, representing many communities, believes that all formation programs should be oriented to this same ultimate end, but it does not presume to legislate what means ought to be adopted by any specific community. The Conference is firmly committed, however, to the view that justice requires every sister who undertakes apostolic work to meet the full standards of pre-service preparation accepted in our society.

The Proceedings and Communications of Regional Meetings of the Sister-Formation Conference are published to serve the ends of Sister Formation but the Conference is obviously not committed to every view which is expressed in the Proceedings.

PRAYER AND RENEWAL

Community and Personal Response to the Spirit

SISTER MARY EVANGELINE McSLOY, R.S.M.
Executive Secretary, Sister Formation Conference

"Response to the Spirit," until the past few years, evoked in most of us a rather peaceful, secure feeling. Perhaps it even brought back memories of generous moments in our lives, moments when we were conscious of our readiness to give, to go to great lengths in order to respond to the Spirit's promptings. When the hierarchy of the Church began to ask for the renewal and adaptations of religious life some years ago, most of us could say that our response was there, and that it was affirmative and positive.

We could agree now, however, that the call to renewal is asking for a response far beyond our most generous calculations, surely greater than any we could have expected. The explanation for this is complex, but very real. Our renewal is taking place while the whole world is in a state of transition—while space and change, communication and travel have made dramatic progress. There is no way of working neatly at renewal, and completing it satisfactorily, as perhaps we had planned; rather, we find ourselves necessarily coping with the issues which everyone in today's world must face, and trying to work realistically through renewal and adaptation of life at the same time.

Today I would like to state positively that I believe that a religious community can indeed work through the problems of renewal satisfactorily. However, because this can be done is no assurance that it *will* be done by a given community. The challenges are steep ones, and the cost, total. It will demand our deepest personal and communal response, and nothing less.

Sometimes when reading history one gets the impression that great souls arise at times when the atmosphere seems least likely to produce them: for example, Francis of Assisi, Francis Borgia, many of our own foundresses. These great persons grew in stature as the times put pressures on them; they could have drifted along under these pressures and become as mediocre as their surroundings invited them to be. Instead, they chose to develop their own powers and to shape their lives. This they did, remaining at the same time people of their own times, with concern for its needs and problems, and with compassion for its people.

The religious communities of our country, then, in response to the Spirit, could today become truly renewed communities. They could become great communities. I believe that this is what the Holy Spirit is urging. But the person and the community must move together. What an agony we experience when individuals truly wish to respond, but the community refuses, or when the majority of the community is responding, and some individuals refuse. This agony, experienced to some degree by every community, I suppose, must not be allowed to continue. There is much that can be done.

One of the strange attitudes that haunts our personalistic age is the pessimistic rationalization about the limits of one person's influence. It is heard in remarks such as: "There is nothing I can do until someone in authority makes a change," or, "No one can do anything until our General Chapter." Now this *is* the age of group action, and as we mentioned, the person and the group should move together. However, we ought not underestimate the power of one person, nor excuse ourselves from maximum effort on the basis of that kind of thinking.

What can,—I would rather say, what *must*—one person do? She must renew her dedication. This only she can do. This means the *giving of oneself*, the handing of oneself over in faith to Christ. And it means living at that level. It means providing the kind of atmosphere of prayer for one's personal life that keeps alive the vision of faith in a world where faith is much in darkness. It means feeding this vision by reading and other means of communication; by sharing ideas with others; by willingness to keep alive mentally, and to continue to learn. All of this demands a personalism that can be defined as a creative way of handling one's real-life situation.

Some kind of intuition tells me that a psychologist would have his own vocabulary for what I have tried to describe: he would call it honest facing up to reality. It is basic to growth of any kind, somewhat painful to bear, but extremely rewarding and satisfying. I do not see how the renewal of our communities can take place unless we are willing to become the kind of persons who are basically sincere and ready to respond as individuals to the message of the Spirit wherever we might find it.

This same sincerity must be the mark of a renewing community; the total community must take the renewal seriously. We blame some of our isolation from one another, our narrowness of vision, on the ascetical practices of the past. That is far too easy to do, and simply another escape for some. Whatever might be the case, *today* we are called to learn again to live the gospel, and to re-learn what it means to be a religious community.

The asceticism demanded is the asceticism of unity. Its vocabulary has been written about and spoken about, so that familiarity with terms may convince us that it is lived. But it is a demanding asceticism; it is based on mutual respect and trust, generous concern shown in listening for the other's truth; unwillingness to judge the other; restraint imposed upon one's selfishness and desire to dominate. In a word, the renewing community must develop anew its inner unity, rebuilding right at the person-to-person level where ruptures may have taken place.

The renewing community must also give its serious attention to the development of its thought, if unity is to be restored and mutual understanding again made possible. Everyone within it must enter into the mutual exchange of ideas, lest anyone become a drag upon the total group. Perhaps this is only a "pet hunch," but I think that there must be those among us with the ability and learning to work with much of what was "traditional" spirituality and/or asceticism of the religious life, and show its relationship to the living of the life today. Each concept would have to be expressed in the kind of thought that fits today's world. Let me give you some examples of ideas which I think are still valid, if really understood and not just considered at a superficial level. It is this lack of understanding and not the concept itself, it seems to me, that is at fault and, therefore, that we must develop, if we are to renew at our roots.

Striving after Perfection: This is one of the "stock" phrases so highly criticized as having led many religious to a dangerous "perfectionism." The phrase really means, . . . not: trying to be "perfect," but, trying to reach, to seek after fulness of love: the life of the love of God and neighbor. The concepts most important to convey here are those of the unrelenting struggle involved in living the ideal of gospel charity. Is this understanding still valid?

Practicing virtue: Here is another culprit. While we may have interpreted this as the repetition of meaningless acts done over and over, did it not really mean developing habits of acting well, responsibly, of making the kinds of choices that are advocated in the gospel and in the lives of great Christians? A person who possesses virtue (power) is a powerful person, one who is trying to become all that she can become by managing her life generously and creatively.

Saying prayers regularly: Here is a great "target." This is a phrase which for many has identified personal growth with mechanical performance. Even Christ Himself criticized those who reduced religion and our relationship to the Lord to mere recitation of formulas. But no great master of prayer that I know of ever equated growth in a spirit of prayer with mere physical presence in a chapel at stated times, though it would be irresponsible to deny the value of some self-discipline. Is it not, perhaps, our own weakness in developing authentic ways of relating our lives to God that has led to an over-dependence upon mechanics? Regularity in prayer is like regularity in life, but not like the regularity of a computer. Perhaps the best remark here might be: we try to computerize in order to control; our relationship with God is a relationship of love, which is never one of domination, but of joyous, free surrender.

These are just a few "snippets" of expressions from our past to show that so much could be done to provide continuity in our thought development. Whole communities should be working together to try to see where present developments began, and how these compare with the true emphasis of the past and present. Often it was our own lack of understanding, or the way in which a truth was presented and lived, that led to weakness or abuses.

One of the characteristics of the call of the Lord in biblical history is the consistent pattern of asking someone or some group to answer "for the sake of others." I cannot think of one person, in the Old or New Testaments, who was called by the Spirit for himself alone.

Religious communities today have a call: they are asked to renew their dedication as persons and as communities for the sake of the whole Church, and of society itself. Christians, indeed all people, are facing the same inner agonies and tensions with which religious communities are struggling. They need the example of persons who believe in and live their dedication, of groups who are determined to succeed in dealing with social change. There was a time when religious communities thought of themselves as giving witness of a perfect community that had solved all its problems, as one that "had it made." Our world needs to see a struggling, human community—but one that has faith and whose members are really trying to live by it. This is the call. How are we going to respond?

Meeting Contemporary Problems and Opportunities in Sister Formation

SISTER M. THOMAS AQUINAS CARROLL, R.S.M.
National Chairman, Sister Formation Conference
Mount Mercy, Pittsburgh, Pennsylvania

In addressing myself to this topic, I am presuming that the Christian message forms the core of our response to everything contemporary. Difficulties and problems echo the Cross: the Cross is the bedrock of our hope; hope turns difficulties into opportunities. My task will be to examine whether we can apply this formula corporately to the business of Sister Formation as each of us knows she can apply it personally. A Christian life without contradiction would belie the words of Christ: "You will be hated by all men on account of my name; but the man who stands firm to the end will be saved." (Matt. 10:22) A Christian life without hardship would make discipleship cheap, whereas Christ has sharply delineated its costliness: "If anyone wants to be a follower of mine, let him renounce himself and take up his cross and follow me. For anyone who wants to save his life will lose it; but anyone who loses his life for my sake will find it." (Matt. 16:24–25)

A Christian life without betrayal would set the servant above the Master, for the Master had his Judas. A Christian life without failure would deprive us of our ultimate Poverty: "Without me you can do nothing,"—and our consequent thirst for prayer.

Let the title of this talk not be lugubrious, then. Problems lead us toward God. They become the ground on which we meet God at a deeper level than ever before. Through the pressures of problems we really engage ourselves, unify our internal powers, learn to concentrate, think through and pray mightily. It is in meeting problems that

6

we grow, grow as decisive, compassionate persons, grow toward God. In God problems become opportunities.

Can a moral person, a religious congregation, or many such, as are here represented similarly grow, in hope, through confrontation of problems to a more authentic and inspiring grasp of opportunities?

When we religious gaily set off three years ago to put in motion the "Adaptation and Renewal" mandated to us by the Second Vatican Council and Pope Paul VI, we forgot momentarily that he who would be reborn must first die. This death has come to us in the shock, the doubts, the fears, the shame that have blasted our self-image as prayerful, mortified, selfless followers of the Lord along the way of the Cross. The fall of structures has carried in its wake the fall of persons. For directors of formation what had seemed solid and time-proven appeared in an unexpected number of sisters to have been conformity rather than true interiorization of values.

This analysis, however, is too rigid, and hence, false.

Rather there was interiorization of values to fit a static church environment, itself out of vital contact with contemporary life and thought. The wrench of assimilating to the Christian message hundreds of years of Western intellectual development formerly isolated and ignored has untidied the system.

Moreover the world society itself is in travail. The Church cannot calmly, with impeccable logic, make choice among static values of a fixed society. Previously non-dominant cultures bid vigorously for a place in the sun. But all, dominant and non-dominant, have been placed on the defensive by a worldwide revolution in the mode of thinking and life-goals acceptable to youth. Experience, embracing the emotions and even the unconscious as well as intellect, replaces dogma, political, economic, and religious, as the master-teacher. Life, *this* life is to be happy and free, and all the forces which obscure this happiness and freedom are to be exorcised.

The climate of opinion in the Church and even in religious congregations has challenged the symbolism, the work, the life-style and even the existence of religious congregations for women. These latter have suffered from the same repercussions as our whole society has. Attacks on institutions, including the Church on all its levels, have dramatized and perhaps deepened cleavages on war and race, poverty, moral standards, individual conscience, and the rights of authority.

The transvaluation of values (to quote Nietzsche) must be worked through anew by each and all of us who prize the Christ-life above all. It is the battle of interiorized values against newly received values, fought within the souls of countless religious, that forms the growth-agony or the death-agony of so many of us. In very large measure the sisters in formation posts have borne the brunt of these problems. Fortunately, as the National Sisters Survey indicates, they were also in the front line of those who understood what was happening in the Church and in the world.

Two years ago in a paper in the *Sister Formation Bulletin* entitled "Everett Revisited," I described the changes which had been accomplished in the formation of sisters in the ten years which had passed since the Everett Curriculum Workshop of 1956. I further outlined the plans which a study committee of the Sister Formation Conference recommended for updating the curriculum for sisters. The workshop envisaged in these plans has not yet materialized.

Individual congregations preempted the time and energies of prospective workshop participants in conducting special chapters of renewal. New pressures from within and outside religious congregations elicited new ways of regarding religious values, apostolates, and, of course, formation. Experimental programs called for moratoria on accepting new members, for the elimination or reduction of the congregation's responsibility for the undergraduate education of its candidates, for the amalgamation of novitiates, for the education of young sisters in secular colleges and universities, and for changes in the time-and-place structuring of formation activities.

Moreover, we began to experience in serious proportions the numbers problem. Withdrawals from the congregations multiplied, new apostolic ventures claimed personnel, and religious vocations decreased sometimes precipitously.

Some would say that the turmoil among us is so great that an organization like the Sister Formation Conference should fold its wings and say *finis*—at least temporarily, leaving the individual congregation to scrutinize its own accomplishments, study its problems and plot its course for the next ten to twelve years. Ultimately the resolution of the Sister Formation Conference depends upon its members. If the sisters feel, as you demonstrate by coming here, that by meeting, discussion, and studying together, we can continue to help each other and thus help individual chapters, the regional conferences will certainly continue. The question remains, however, whether in addition to the on-going resolution of current problems, we can also turn these problems into opportunities and bring forth, as a national body as well as individually, the energy, psychic and spiritual, to confront opportunities and weld them into a new program as effective in its way as was Everett of 1956.

NUMBERS

Let us look then at some of the problems-to-be-converted-into-opportunities. The shrinkage of numbers in our formation programs confronts us on all sides. Large beautiful buildings, many of them new, become purveyors of gloom when they are only one-third occupied. The extensive farmland grounds appear frivolous when a handful of sisters uses them and a handicap when education-where-the-action-is becomes a goal. I have no solution to the real-estate problem. But a conference of major superiors of men and women, of bishops with seminaries on their hands, along with a group of real-estate specialists might well help one another to realistic and future-oriented decisions. Our purpose is rather to study these buildings in the light of formation needs. Did their quality of "cloistered elegance" and self-sufficiency impart the climate conducive to growth in concern for the world, selflessness, participation in the woes and agonies of mankind? Was the quiet which nature offered as an invitation to thoughtfulness and prayer offset by the beehive-like organization of numbers within? Did the group orientation and the limited freedom allow personality defects to escape unnoticed, or to go by unplumbed? Is there a quality of selfhood lost when a young person becomes too totally part of an institution? Can we look at the emptiness of our new and mortgaged buildings not with despair but with that trust in God that can read His signs? Let us look at this decline in number of candidates as a sign from God and see what He may be saying.

Frequently studies of the Old Testament point out that the great spiritual achievements of the Hebrews occurred at periods when external circumstances made life hard and unrewarding. Eras of calm, peace, and prosperity lulled the Chosen People into a superficial security where a covenant with God seemed unnecessary and unexciting. I am not at all implying that religious have not been faithful to their covenant. What I am saying is that we may use our present hiatus as a providentially given time to search our values: our values of prestige and comfort, of order and precision, of form and routine. Sense-deprivation or sense-development: for which are we striving? Do we trust too much to the environment to make the person? Do we conceive of interiorization of values as automatic? Have we tried to do too much on a supernatural level without an adequate underpinning in the natural order? Even when we succeeded, was our prayerful, disciplined religious out-of-tune with her culture?

What we may use our time for is better diagnosis of needs. Do we need small-group living? Do we need dispersion of peer groups? Do we need one-to-one master-disciple relationships? Can we use institutional living, can we adapt it, or must we discard such structures altogether?

The decline in numbers may present a temptation to decrease or eliminate formation personnel. Here again planning becomes the essential element. If such a reduction of personnel arises simply from the shortage of sisters to fulfill other apostolic commitments it is shortsighted. In this case it might lead to a return to the days when one religious was charged with the entire formation complex from postulancy to final vows. On the other hand, a philosophy might be adopted of making every member of the congregation responsible for the formation of the young members. Buried here is the hope of renewing all the sisters, and of course the danger also of exploiting the new recruit. I think primarily of emotional exploitation. But also forcibly to be warned against is the introduction of the young sister into professionally demanding works in roles for which she is not academically prepared. Despite small numbers we must not be sparing in the sisters who can give themselves primarily to formation activities. Perhaps for their own development and the enhancement of their work some part-time assignment to the apostolate is valid. My chief contention is that probably the ratio of our formation personnel to our young sisters needs to be higher than ever before.

The lack of adequate personnel to meet apostolic commitments—indeed a grievous problem—may be converted into an opportunity. When our decision makers face the fact that they really cannot continue all the current engagements their congregations have undertaken, they become, in a sense, freed, and mentally forced to identify more clearly which are the most fruitful apostolates where each sister may make her best contribution. And they can then take active measures towards collaboration, collaboration in apostolic ventures; collaboration even in formation ventures. Where numbers are sparse, we cannot overlook the reassurance value of having our young sister meet postulants and novices of other congregations, and know that though in different families, they too are attempting to answer the call of the Lord to celibate community.

CHANGE

In addition to the numbers problem, we must face the fact that our former formation structures prepared for a fairly static religious congregation in a static Church. Rules were looked upon as final, sacred to their last syllable. The first time it was suggested by the Sacred Congregation of Religious that our constitutions should be changed, a real trauma was experienced, a blow to security from which some of us have never recovered. We had ignored the fact that, actually, the meaning of the Holy Rule had been systematically choked by the addition of long passages from canon law, for these had come from "the Church." It had not occurred to us that *we* should change the rule! What a revolution has occurred! We must become the makers of our constitutions, and we must build change into them if they are to be of enduring value. We must strive by the very rules we adopt to keep ourselves open to change, for only thus will we be able to live in a changing Church, in a changing world, and fulfill therein, vital roles. We must know, therefore, what we are about. We must plumb the Gospel, our traditions and the world's needs to express our essence. We must accept diversity in form and flexibility in approach, in every phase of our life together.

To build community on the twin pillars of adaptability to change and diversity requires that we study long and hard the primacy of charity and its rootedness in personhood, that we be willing to recast and enlarge our own thinking to embrace our sister lovingly within it. We must change our perceptions to adjust to the Church's own view of herself—no longer as transcendent, triumphal, perfect, but as a pilgrim toiling painfully through a history made sinful by her members. If we adopt this view how gladly will we accept the helping hand of our sister even if she does not fit our version of the perfect religious, if her stance is casual and her manner free, and even if she asks impertinent questions about our aged customs. If we're on a journey we can't afford burdensome baggage: it may handicap our preservation of the essentials. Discovering the essentials by removing forms can become a unifying bond for those really seeking true community in Christ.

Prominent among the challenges of our society is that of the nature and exercise of authority, and its correlative, obedience. The sister acutely conscious of her personhood reacts badly to obedience formulated on some artificially allotted status such as junior. She is willing to give obedience to God; she is willing to try to live a Gospel life; she is willing to accept obedience for apostolic purposes in a professionally regulated structure, but obedience for obedience's sake arouses no response. What areas are here revealed for theological analysis, psychological probing, direction, and discernment of spirits! How beautifully, though, can this problem of our young become an opportunity for all of us to question our authority–obedience structures to allow for the creativity, flexibility, and initiative the needs of our world-society require!

The contemporary problem with permanent commitment plagues bishops and higher superiors with misgivings about the image of the Church, the continuance of the works of the Church, her continued sacramental life, her very existence. And yet formation personnel must admit that this very uncertainty of permanent commitment adds dimension to every facet of their work—a dimension which can be made an opportunity for taking a harder look at basic motivation, penetrating more deeply into personality development, laboring more over growth in personal prayer-life, wanting to see each person as utterly free as possible before she makes binding decisions. Freedom attains a much greater prominence as a goal when measured in the context of the questioning of permanent commitment. We lose our concern, even our desire for protective cloisters of any type. We find ourselves wanting our young sisters to have any experiences which will prevent a collapse after final vows. Not that we tempt them to throw away chances of successful religious vocation, but we allow them to test themselves in freedoms which at once measure and strengthen their deep purpose towards consecration.

That contemporary youth is "different," I'm sure we shall also agree. I hope though we will be equally emphatic that this difference also affords us a magnificent opportunity. Our youth are masters in the art of "turning off." And by this technique they have made us defensive, self-critical, and willing to seek new means to win their involvement. They learn differently. We took it for granted that civilized people learned from laws, from books, from example; but for them experience is the one sure teacher. By this single difference a generation gap of incalculable depth is created, and formation programs proven by the centuries are defeated. A cultural revolution of proportions unprecedented in history has been effected. And relationship to God is not the least of the values affected.

Within a religious community, as within the Church and all of society, because of this cultural hiatus, the evil to be fought is polarization. Can we use the newness of our young members so as not to polarize them from the fixed, statically good sisters, but to renew the whole congregation? Can we build upon the newly valued personalism to develop mutual respect, love and trust based simply upon the fact that *we are*, that God loves us enough to make us and give us a future with Him? Can we evolve new structures based upon open search together, frank honesty, loving acceptance of ourselves as limited and fallible and sinful? Can we admit the "surprise beat" of current culture into the stately forms of our daily living? Will we bend to our youth to freshen and purify our own concepts and then challenge them on their own faulty assumptions? Shall we understand them enough to see through their brashness to the groping, pleading quest beneath? Shall we make of our differences a bridge of strength or a gully of despair?

EDUCATION

The contemporary problems of formation within our communities are indeed staggering. Yet they must never occupy us to the point that we lose sight of the contribution which intellectual formation must also make. It was in this field that Sister Formation Conference achieved revolutionary results. If only we had also all paid attention to the full program of the Sister Formation Conference leaders, including spiritual-formation teams, attention to the behavioral sciences, and a Sister Formation Committee to help to integrate the educational and the spiritual! However, much remains to be done, even within the educational area. The institutions in which we educate our sisters must be continuously evaluated. Whether they be our own, those of other religious orders, or state colleges, we must insist upon using only regionally accredited ones. We never were able to afford poor units of higher education; even less so can we now, with so much pressure for higher standards and with the rampant criticism of our works. Let us give each other the courage to move in this matter; in being harsh let us be realistically kind.

In the interests of maturity and economy, some congregations are admitting only applicants who have completed baccalaureate education. Others continue to accept applicants after the completion of high school or intermediate periods of college work. For all, my plea is that they provide a sound doctrinal education. Surely every sister should have the equivalent of an academic major in sound religious studies, particularly Sacred Scripture and Christology. Beyond this, it seems to me that it should become a vocational goal of the Sister Formation Conference, that every sister before, or shortly after her final consecration, should have a year or two of advanced doctrinal study, where she might gain some initiation and insight into the method of the theologian. Of immense help to her at this point would be continued work in ecclesiology. Without doubt, it is in the field of religious studies that the sister will be most needed in the future. In fact we will probably see the day when some such doctrinal study will be taken for granted in the preparation of a sister as is done today before the ordination of a priest. Not that every sister will be a theologian, or a specialist in religion but that every sister will be expected to meet and to deal adequately with adults. The sister social worker, nurse, first-grade teacher, the teenage recreation director will need this level of doctrinal proficiency. The teacher of catechetics, the professor of religion will of course need much more, and more scholarly preparation. In fact, as we face the realities of our pluralistic society, we may accept as our fundamental criterion: "How do we educate the sister to dialogue with an atheist?"

Facing such a challenge can we not turn each of our difficulties into an opportunity?

The Woodstock Conference
Consensus Statement*

Sister Formation Conference
Woodstock Workshop
June 23 to July 8, 1968

"The Sister Formation Conference sponsored a workshop during this past year for personnel involved in the formation of sisters. Participants in the workshop formulated the following consensus report which they desired to have transmitted to members of the Conference of Major Superiors of Women.

"The leadership meeting of the Sister Formation Conference considered this statement at length and decided to transmit it intact to the major superiors. In doing this, the leadership group wishes to make it clear that it does not consider the Woodstock statement as conclusive or definitive. Some elements in it appear excellent in thrust and insight, others lack clarity; some suggestions have been universalized beyond their desert, some recommendations may even be found to be ill-advised. Each major superior is urged to study the whole statement carefully, however, as one attempt to answer the questions over which formation personnel are sincerely agonizing, and weigh each part in terms of its local applicability.

"The leadership group commends the workshop participants for their enthusiasm for the vitality of religious life, their concern to make its essential elements relevant to its young recruits, and their confidence in receiving a hearing from their major superiors."

* The following report is printed here, in accordance with the wishes of those who prepared it, entirely without editing. The text is preceded, however, by the statement which the Leadership Meeting prepared to send with it to the Conference of Major Superiors of Women. (ed.)

PREAMBLE

The following statements represent the consensus of the participants in a two-week workshop on formation of Sisters, held at Woodstock College, Maryland, June 23 to July 8, 1968, at the direction of and under the sponsorship of the Leadership Group of the Sister Formation Conference.

Some 95 communities participated in the project by submitting to the workshop descriptions of their present formation programs, changes projected for the future, and the thinking underlying these steps. These reports formed the background material for the workshop discussions.

About 150 sisters from 96 communities participated in the workshop itself, including 16 sisters still in formation as junior professed, novices, or candidates. The participants were drawn from every geographical area of the United States and, while the majority consisted of persons with substantial experience in formation work, the broader range of community life and experience was evidenced by the presence and participation of hospital administrators and personnel, college, high-school and elementary administrators, vocational personnel, major and local superiors, and sisters on mission assignments. The participants were assisted in their deliberations by resource personnel in the fields of history, ascetical, biblical, and systematic theology, psychology, psychiatry, and counseling. Their discussion was further challenged by the presence of representatives of the Jesuit Community of Woodstock College, of the community of Taizé, the Focolare Movement, a Peace Corps training director, and the regional couple of the Équipes-Notre Dame for the field of conjugal spirituality.

No one of the participants is empowered to speak for her community and therefore these statements do not pretend to "represent" in a juridical way the communities involved in the project. Nor can they claim to be a position adopted by the Sister Formation Conference as such. They are offered rather as a service to all the religious communities of women in the United States, with whatever suasive power people will find in such a gathering, meeting in such a fashion and with such resources at this hour in the history of religious life in the United States.

PRAYER

Prayer is variously described as encounter with God, contact with God, awareness of God, experience of God. All these descriptions involve God's revealing His presence to a person and that person's response. God is free to reveal Himself as He wishes. This revelation may occur in such situations as solitary reflection, community living, reading of the Word of God, Eucharistic liturgy, common prayer, services, encounters with others, apostolic action. The conclusion, loving response to God's presence in any of these life situations is prayer. This is not to say that work is prayer nor that solitary reflection is prayer, though both are good and both are necessary to man and both are vital expressions of the Christian life, and both *can* lead to prayer. Prayer is then the conscious, loving response to God's presence whether He reveals Himself to the eyes of faith in the transparency of an event or a person, or in solitary reflection.

Sensitive to the need for both involvement and reflection, the person should avoid making an idol either of immersion in the world or of solitude. Both can be engaged in, without praying. Overemphasis on immersion in the world runs the risk of a person's being overwhelmed by his activities and experiences so that reality becomes opaque and conceals God from man. Overemphasis on solitary reflection runs the risk of degenerating into self-delusion and a flight from the real. The Christian will try to remain open to all the *loci* of God's self-manifestations, realizing therefore the value and the need for involvement in the world of human events, community life, personal encounter with others, the liturgy, para-liturgical common prayer, and in solitude. The particular personality of the sister, her life situation and vocational commitment will determine in broad lines the particular configuration of these events in the rhythm of her life. This configuration makes up the context in which she responds to the initiative of the Holy Spirit in her life. In this sense, it is the basis of her spirituality, of the openness of her person to the influence of the Spirit of Christ. It is the milieu in which she takes on the mind and heart of Christ and relives in her own unique way the Paschal Mystery of the Lord.

In the most profound sense of the word, the style of her prayer is rooted in the depth of her person. Her prayer is one of the deepest expressions of who she is. For this reason she needs the freedom to see God in the way best adapted to her present self with all the dimensions that go to make her who she is. Therefore, there is no need to overemphasize fixed structures of prayer. As she assimilates the spirit of her community, it cannot but be expressed in her prayer. Her experience of life in community—in the Church and more particularly in her religious community—will enrich her person and therefore enhance her prayer and give it a particular tonality.

SPIRITUAL DIRECTION

By spiritual direction the religious seeks to make an authentic response to the stirrings of the Holy Spirit. The principal concern, then, is the discernment of spirits. While this discernment is ultimately the affair of the individual religious under the influence of the Holy Spirit, it is always carried on in the context of real life, in vital contact with the people and the events that make up her world. She may at times seek the assistance of a competent person, whether priest, religious, or lay, to help her in the task of discernment. Though she may draw assistance from others, the final responsibility for the direction of her life is her own.

Recommendations (prayer and spiritual direction)

It is recommended:

1. That religious communities encourage creativity on the part of individual members and local communities in planning a meaningful liturgy which is in basic solidarity with the Church.
2. That opportunities for varied experiences in contemporary forms of communal prayer be made available to all sisters (e.g. occasional community meditations, Bible services, penance liturgies, experiments with the office).
3. That communities be encouraged to consider these new insights into the dispositions for prayer, namely:
   a) renunciation as availability to God's call;
   b) silence as active listening to reality;

   c) solitude as having enough space to be oneself;

   d) recollection as being "all there" where one is.

4. That the community policy manifest a concern for the sisters' need for new approaches to retreat, days of renewal, and that the individual sister, taking into consideration both her own needs and those of the community, be free to make appropriate choices of time, place, and form.

5. That personal prayer be nourished primarily by the Word of God and the liturgy.

6. That formation personnel be competent primarily in the area of spiritual guidance and secondarily in counseling. This requires formal training in current theology and in counseling skills.

PERSON AND COMMUNITY

Introduction:

American sisters today have no deeper yearning than to take their place within the entire people of God, in the mission of the Church on behalf of the human person and human community, and in the secular struggle to build a better world for all men everywhere. They conceive this investment in the future of the world as an integral part of their dedication to the coming of the Kingdom of God. They are convinced that the religious life when really lived in its fulness, has a distinctive contribution to make to this great human task of our times. They are aware that they, like the Church itself, will be judged by God and by posterity on their persevering willingness to accept this call of the Spirit.

American sisters reject, therefore, any structure or any attitude in themselves or in others which would imply that by their consecration, religious women "become strangers to their fellow men or useless citizens of this earthly city." (*Lumen gentium*, ch. 46) They wish to cooperate with the clergy, with the rest of the laity, and with men of good will generally, to create within and around their communities an environment which will foster the fullest possible growth of each person and further the fuller achievement of deep and radiant human and Christian community.

American sisters, especially in their chapters of renewal, are envisaging their lives more and more in terms of person in community. They relate this vision to the universal struggle on behalf of the human person and the community of mankind. The following reflections and recommendations offer not so much new insight as an encouraging witness to what we have learned from other sisters and from one another during this workshop.

No brief statement can presume to express the depth and richness of the mystery of the person and the mystery of the community, especially as seen in the light of the Paschal Mystery. Neither can it convey the precise accents and nuances called for in various concrete situations within communities widely differing in traditions and life styles. Nor can delicate balances and tensions (for example, between individual and community, between inward- and outward-looking aspects of life in apostolic community) be captured in a single formula.

Our sharing on the theme of person and community has given us the fresh and joyous realization that in our Father's house there are many mansions, that the one Spirit bestows a wide diversity of gifts, and that there is an infinite variety of forms, life styles and accents possible in the realization of celibate Christian community on behalf of the human person and the community of mankind. What must be common to all our efforts is a passion for the dignity, freedom and growth of the human person, a passion for the unity of all men in Christ, and passion for the new world founded on truth, directed by justice realized in freedom, motivated by love, and flowering in peace.

Statement

In the communitarian life of the Trinity, the fullness of personality is realized. Christ, "the Man for others," incarnates Presence to the Other by reconciling man to the Father and with each other through the power of the Spirit. The Church, the Sacrament of Christ's reconciling presence to and in the world, commits herself to a dialogue-partnership with the world on behalf of person and community. This commitment is credible and effective only in fidelity to the Paschal Mystery and to continuing inner renewal.

Religious life is a distinctive way of living the Paschal Mystery. Celibate Christian community, through its consecration, witness, and service, provides complementarity for the primary secular Christian community, the family. By witnessing to the Paschal Mystery through the evangelical counsels, by constant inner renewal, and by relevant service to person and community, religious life manifests its authenticity.

Celibate love in seeking the realization of the total Christ is the bond of religious community. The expression of love in community is mutual sensitivity to the needs of the others, mutual acceptance of the uniqueness of the other, and mutual availability and concern for the other. Diversity of means creatively serves unity.

A religious community and its individual members respond dynamically to the signs of the times by a blending and balancing of:

a) Celebration of life, both personal and communal;
b) Radical opposition to evil;
c) Reform of attitudes and structures hindering individual and social development;
d) Professional excellence.

Basic to responding dynamically to the signs of the times is the continual evaluation of the community's witness to the gospel values and continual adaptation of the means of their expression. Integral to this is the honest assessment of policies and practices in the light of theological, technological, cultural, and social changes in the modern world.

Dialogue-partnership with the modern world demands frequent interaction between the religious community and secular agencies. In order to achieve within the community the awareness of and participation in this involvement, inter- and intra-community communications must be constant.

Recommendations

It is recommended:

1. That the members of each community seek to re-create it as a community of continual evangelical conversion by such means as:
   a) Studying and deepening its expression of evangelical values;
   b) Celebration of meaningful liturgies and frequent reflection on the Word of God;
   c) Creative employment of communication and discussion;
   d) In-service education so that all members may more fully participate in community renewal.

2. That the sisters of each community seriously examine its present laws, customs, institutions, and style of living to see whether they are fully compatible with the dignity of the person as described in the documents of Vatican II and the encyclicals of Popes John XXIII and Paul VI. The community's own profile, as revealed by the Sisters' Survey, should be made available to each sister, and be interpreted and utilized by the community for this end.

3. That every community continue to educate each member towards responsible action in her personal decisions, and to encourage each person to use her creative initiative in developing her community as a dynamic force in society.

4. That each community seriously examine the possible ways in which, as a celibate Christian community, it may more fully share mutual witness and dialogue with the community of Christian marriage and family.

5. That charity characterize the community's relations with sisters who withdraw from it, both before and after their actual departure.

6. That each community, according to its basic spirit and style of life, accentuate the value of appropriate participation by individual members in other forms of religious and secular community.

7. That the sharing of community life and facilities with others be regarded as a powerful aid to personal growth and community spirit, provided it takes place with discretion and with sensitivity to the needs and desires of all members.

INCORPORATION INTO THE CONGREGATION

Introduction:

Owing to general cultural conditions of today, adulthood is reached at a later time. For the most part, it is recognized that sufficient life experience is necessary before a person can make a free choice of life direction. Adulthood in our society is manifested by independence, initiative, ability to handle change, potential to respond to reality-factors of one's situation, capacity to form true love-relationships, and the inner drive toward growth and freedom.

Our society is characterized by rapid change, instability and insecurity. It is possible to view persons developing in that society in terms of three general responses: those open and anxious to participate in a changing world, those fearing it and wishing to withdraw to a place of security, those fearing change but willing to participate in and shape the evolving world. The particular characteristics of a specific congregation will determine the type of person who will be attracted to that congregation.

A fruitful encounter between the congregation and the young women who are the candidates of today can happen only if both congregation and candidate honestly engage in dialogue. (The term candidate refers to the whole period of incorporation prior to final commitment.) Both must have realistic expectations of each other.

The congregation's part in this honest dialogue is a preliminary evaluation of its own goals and aspirations to see if they are consonant with the goals and aspirations that motivate the people of our time. It must also test out the characteristic manner in which it tries to achieve its goals and aspirations. The structures it uses will have to become more flexible so that free, independent young women can thrive within them.

The candidate herself, if she is to be honest in her part of the dialogue, must be aware of her need to change and accept the values of the congregation as well as its present reality. This will be possible only if the atmosphere within the congregation not only allows but encourages personal responsibility, initiative, critical evaluations; in short, those values in which the young have learned to flourish. She can learn to accept the community as it is to the degree that the community can accept her.

Preparation of the Candidate

The purpose of the program is to provide the candidate with the preparation that is necessary for a life of authentic consecration and service. Preparation for life and work in a religious congregation should take place within a context as realistic as possible. It would seem that this preparation would best take place in the context of a community of professed sisters where there is an awareness of current human needs and the opportunity to respond to them. The philosophy of the program should be positive and should communicate confidence in the ability of the adult person to continue self-initiated growth. The program should provide for:

a) Development of the person to that degree of maturity that will enable her to make a lifetime dedication;
b) Opportunity to deepen Christian life;
c) Opportunities to include within the context of her dedication response to the needs of mankind and a willingness to join men of good will in their efforts to achieve social justice, peace, unity;
d) Opportunities to deepen appreciation of central values of the congregation and to grow in commitment to them;
e) Professional competence.

Role of the Local Community

The Spirit inspires and graces each person so her response is like to that of no other. While respecting the movement of the Spirit within each member, the Congregations must also provide experienced personnel who will assist the candidates to genuine self-direction. In addition, the Congregation, recognizing the dynamic presence of the Spirit in its own midst, must urge all its members to assume a more active and responsible role in creating an atmosphere and building attitudes conducive to growth in the Spirit.

In this perspective, the local community assumes its proper role in the preparation of the candidate. Through sincere discussion it should make explicit the source of unity in the Congregation and recognize that a variety of responses is not only compatible with but also enriches this unity.

With the above in mind each community within the Congregation should study:

1) Its readiness and ability to accept a candidate living in the world of rapid change;
2) The type of incorporation program to be adopted, taking into consideration the uniqueness of the person seeking incorporation, and the goals of the Congregation;
3) The amount of flexibility that is possible regarding time, place, duration, and content of the initial period;
4) The manner in which the candidates will participate in decisions that affect community life and work;
5) The form of commitment before permanent consecration;

6) The means of identifying with the world around them and concerning themselves with the needs of their fellowmen;

7) The ways and means for examining and evaluating its effectiveness in carrying out its goals so that there will be a constant, responsible, creative inner renewal of each member and therefore, of the entire community.

Means of Incorporation

The gradual incorporation of the candidate into the Congregation will continue until such time as the candidate, the formation personnel, and those members of the Congregation who have lived with her agree that she is ready to make a lifetime dedication.

Religious women of today should inaugurate with confidence a serious study of the best possible expression of their permanent and personal commitment to Christ. It is clear that the three evangelical vows of poverty, chastity, and obedience are one of the traditional forms of complete dedication to a Gospel way of life within the Church. This is not to say, however, that this is the only way or necessarily the way that the Spirit will lead us in the future. Each Congregation is encouraged, through its general chapter, to study various expressions of commitment in view of the eventual adoption of that form which best expresses its own charism. This study is prompted by a desire to be faithful to the conciliar call for renewal in all areas.

Only by creating a climate of genuine trust, openness, and dialogue can sisters eventually come to realize and accept their responsible role in preparing candidates for perpetual commitment. At each stage of incorporation, the entire Congregation—the major superior and her council, sisters in the community, formation personnel, and each sister in the initial stages of incorporation—with and in Christ, under the movement of the Spirit, seeks to discover the Father's will. Together they can accept the challenge to search for new forms of living the radical message of Christianity.

CONCLUSIONS AND RECOMMENDATIONS

Because the readiness of the Congregation is a major factor in the successful incorporation of candidates, some of these conclusions deal with attitudes and values which affect such readiness.

1. In general, entrance immediately after high school is not advisable. It is recommended that the candidate have sufficient life experience to enable her to achieve something of an adult identity.

2. An important dimension of the formation of a candidate is involvement in the apostolic endeavors of the congregation. The degree of involvement should be determined by her personal needs and professional competency. Expediency should never be the deciding factor. The assumption of a professional role without proper credentials for professional service violates social justice and must not be tolerated.

3. Forms of isolation and withdrawal based on pre-conciliar theology and conspicuous during the initial phases of incorporation, are no longer valid. Each member should therefore assume personal responsibility for keeping abreast of the changing vision of our world through intelligent use of modern communications media such as literature, news coverage, art, music, films and drama.

4. It is necessary to demythologize many of our institutions and practices, e.g., (1) religious as a privileged class, (2) the dual-merit theory for persons with vows, (3) the grace of office, (4) certain concepts of obedience, (5) vows as ends in themselves.

5. Each congregation should know its CMSW Sisters' Survey profile and develop its formation and renewal programs accordingly.

6. In view of the question of authoritarianism raised by this Survey and keeping in mind the thrust of conciliar theology, each congregation should create governmental structures to incorporate:
   a) Genuine decentralization of authority;
   b) actual adherence to the principle of subsidiarity;
   c) room for personal freedom and responsibility.

7. Adoption of collegial structures of life and government necessitates corresponding alterations in the practical living out of one's commitment.

8. If we accept in principle that there will be a variety of ways of expressing the basic values operative in a particular congregation, then we must be ready to accept the fact that there may be sisters who wish to engage in poverty programs, demonstrations, political activities, and other forms of social involvement including,

perhaps, the most controversial. Participation in these programs will sometimes necessitate new forms of community living.

9. Rather than legislate in the area of personal decision and choices, the congregation should encourage individual members and communities to act responsibly and to be willing to live with all the consequences of their choices, including failure. In both success and failure the individual person and the community should be assured of support.

10. In determining and executing their policies, congregations should engage in on-going consultation with persons outside the congregation.

11. Readiness for renewal implies both education and implementation; courageous implementation accompanied by communication is often a most effective way of educating.

12. The congregation which moves from a structure-centered life to a person-centered life must employ massive and effective communication both horizontal and vertical, to achieve and maintain unity.

13. Religious congregations should extend understanding and support in a special way to the efforts of other congregations to respond to the conciliar call for renewal.

GENERAL RECOMMENDATIONS

The 1968 Sister Formation Workshop recommends:

1. That the CMSW express to the bishops their eagerness to improve communications between local religious and their bishop, and proceed to arrange meetings on the national and local levels at which there would be religious superiors, representatives chosen by the community, bishops and their vicars for religious. Among the topics to the discussed at these meetings are: full liturgical life, canonical examination and visitation, diocesan counselling service, and issues that impede harmonious cooperation. It is further recommended that the CMSW ask Bishop Breitenbeck to inform the bishops to anticipate requests for these meetings.

2. That the CMSW stimulate its members to share with the bishops the decrees of their General Chapters. The necessity for valid experimentation requires that those involved be informed.

3. That the CMSW encourage its membership to create within their respective communities, channels for effective communication, sharing with all the members the activities, the concerns, and the communiqués from the Conference and from other sources which provide information helpful for religious life.

4. That representatives from the 1968 Sister Formation Workshop meet with the members of the executive board of CMSW from their region to communicate to them the outcomes of the Workshop.

5. That a delegation of Sisters representing the 1958 Sister Formation Workshop inform the September meeting of CMSW of the recommendations of the Workshop.

6. That the major superiors together with some formation personnel communicate the results of the 1968 Sister Formation Workshop to the Episcopal Commission on Religious Life at an acceptable time before the November meeting of the bishops.

7. That the trends in formation of women religious indicated at the 1968 Sister Formation Workshop be disseminated on the local and national levels by mass media.

The 1968 Sister Formation Workshop wished to express its appreciation and its support for the continued efforts of the CMSW in regard to the revision of Canon Law.

Panel on the Woodstock Paper

COMMENT

Sister Mary Finn
Home Visitors of Mary
Detroit, Michigan

I PRAYER

Language is a carrier of meanings and values. What I mean and value lives and hides in the words I speak, the pictures I draw, the gestures I make, the songs I sing, the sculptures I shape. Whether I know it consciously or not my language both hides and discloses the deepest and most hidden roots and movements of my personality. Language tells you and hides from you what I mean and where I am going. My language discloses the hidden shape of my life. Out of the heart my tongue speaks. When my language is precise you say I "tell it like it is."

The question is: Does the Woodstock Statement on Prayer "tell it like it is"? I am not going to elaborate on content or style. Style is relative. Content you have available before you. In these few moments I invite you not merely to interpret, but to explore and question what is carried in the language of the statement on Prayer, and discover what is actually hidden *in* and what is hidden *by* its language. To do this it would be helpful for you to: first of all, know the origin of the statement; secondly, recall your own experience of reading the statement. Then we are able to unveil implications—those meanings hidden beneath language; and fourthly, to appreciate the statement on prayer in a new way.

First, the origin of the statement: the statement on Prayer originated fundamentally and immediately out of a lecture given at Woodstock by the Rev. Ernest Larkin and remarks by the Rev. Daniel Foley, S.J., on spiritual direction. The language of both men is faithful to our Western preference for the academic and logical, and to our contemporary preoccupation with freedom and individuality. It is a language of the head more than the heart, so the statement may read like a "brainstorm"—like a collection of thoughts and ideas on prayer—and not an experience of prayer. It informs "about" prayer, but is unlikely to inspire prayer. It is instructional; more an explanation than an inspiration to pray. Unless my words "about" prayer carry my religious experience of God they may be academic words and non-inspirational. Academics of prayer is different from prayer. Whenever I pray I experience myself "centering." My center is not me. My center is Christ. My center is the Father. I am gathered together, united, centered with Them and Their Spirit. In Them I move in and toward harmony with myself, with my associates, with things and events around me. As soon as I try to "explain" my experience of prayer or describe my centering, I move away from the core of religious experience itself—somewhat like laughter or weeping. As soon as I try to "explain" my sorrow or joy to you, I move away from my experience of it. The experience of praying is interrupted by brainstorming about prayer—but then, to brainstorm about prayer is quite typically twentieth-century American.

The statement says "prayer is the conscious loving response to God's presence" in a life situation. Among the various life situations at Woodstock was the presence of Father Larkin and Father Foley. The statement on Prayer appears as a response to their presence—and insofar as it is, it is a contribution to the study of prayer, and is also a contribution by revealing a dearth of initiative and creativity—perhaps even a lack of resourcefulness and prayerfulness in the life of the participants. It is one of the limitations of the statement that it reflects so extensively the thought and academic system of a few, rather than the religious experience of the speakers and participants. The statement is "local" and "Woodstocky," because there is little trace in the language of any roots that go much deeper than the mechanics and human relations of Woodstock, and the day or so of writing the statement. This happened partly because it was put together with haste, and without recourse to the deep inner life and prayer experience of the writers. It lacks "soul";—but it is difficult to get "soul" into a "consensus statement."

Secondly, recall your own feeling-response as you read the statement. Did what you read correspond at all to your own experience of the Lord? In other words: would you recognize the experience you call "prayer" from what you read? Were you inspired to pray, or intellectually exercised? There is a difference. Did you sense any bias or defense in the persons behind the statement, any effort to prove a point about person and freedom and community living?

Thirdly, and at the heart of this discussion, is the invitation to explore implications—not merely to interpret, but to make explicit what is actually said in the statement but is hidden *in* and *by* its language.

In one sense the Woodstock statement on prayer does not "tell it like it is." In language it is vague, marginal, ambiguous, elusive, out of the mind. In another sense, the statement really does "tell it like it is" because it discloses almost exactly what our everyday cultural experience is: obsession, preoccupation, fascination with human values.

Fundamentally, the language of the statement is *man*-centered and discloses to us how very functional and scientific we are—how profound we are theologically; how deprived we are spiritually. In the statement the "center" of the prayer experience is ambiguous. It shifts between God and man. There are various hidden implications that prayer is more a human experience than a religious experience. The person of man, more than the Persons of God emerges as the center of prayer. Quite consistently "she," "her personality" is primary. *She* encounters God. "*Her* personality, life situation, vocational commitment are the basis of spirituality." "*She* takes on the mind and the heart of Christ." *She* relives in her own way the Paschal Mystery. "The style of her prayer is rooted in the depth of *her* person. Her prayer is one of the deepest expressions of who *she* is." *She* needs freedom to seek God in the very best way adapted to *her* present self with all that makes her who she is. Her experience of life will enrich her person and enhance her prayer. The section on Spiritual Direction says discernment of the spirit is "ultimately the affair of the individual."

This language discloses a searching concern for the dignity and development of the human personality. Language also suggests this statement is actually not a statement on "prayer" as much as it is on freedom of person in community. Implied in the language is the power *she* has to control her "conscious loving response to God"—to control her prayer and her God. It suggests that human personality dominates the Spirit. Human personality determines what God will do for me, so prayer occurs more at man's initiative than God's. The statement is more psychological than spiritual; prayer more a psychological experience than an enriching spiritual experience—more human spirit–centered than Holy Spirit centered. Language even implies something magical as, if one does "all this" she will be praying.

For all the contemporary insistence about person-centeredness this statement misses the person-ness of God. In language it is actually impersonal when it comes to God. God is objectivated—out there "in the world of human events," "community life," "encounter with others," "apostolic action." There is little inspiration in the statement to meet God as Person and experience His own personality as Father, as Son, as Spirit.

The language of the statement, especially the section on spiritual direction, and in the recommendations insists that religious be treated as personal. But this very insistence is expressed impersonally. A discontinuity appears between the implications of the text and implications of the recommendations. The text appeals to the individual. Recommendations appeal to *community* and have more to do with "personal freedom in community" than prayer and religious experience.

The language of recommendation #3, for example, makes explicit the role of the Community in fostering renunciation, silence, solitude, recollection—but hardly even implies that these dispositions and experiences originate by the action of the Lord in person.

Recommendation #6 discloses the need for "training" formation personnel in the theology and counseling skills. It is striking there is no reference to the spiritual prayer-life of the formation personnel. The implication for the formation personnel in this recommendation is similar to the implication for all religious in the entire statement: that the academics of prayer are central. There is little appeal to formation personnel to unfold their own personal presence before the Lord and their experience of the Lord to the initiate. To summarize this section: the Woodstock Statement on Prayer did the "traditional" thing: suggested horizontal renewal, expansion at the surface. We came to Woodstock in need of *vertical* renewal. Woodstock '68 was not yet ready to move vertically, but has perhaps inspired us to do so.

Fourthly, we appreciate the Woodstock Statement on Prayer. It implies reverence for personal presence, freedom and community. We appreciate it because it reveals how dry and deprived we are in religious experience; shows our bias toward man centeredness, and discloses our fascination with human values. Any statement that is this full is a contribution, and an invitation to growth. In this sense we are able to be critical of it. It is meant to go beyond its present moment. The statement is valued, because it enables us to name a few limitations, to uncover a few hidden implications. Man cannot see or say "all things all at once." John does not say all there is to be said about Christ. Perhaps the Christ John experiences is not experienced by Matthew. Woodstock likewise, speaks a few words, intellectualizes a few sides of religious experience, touches a few levels of the Lord's revealing presence. When I know only the Christ John knows I do violence to Christ and to John. When I know only the Woodstock '68 description of prayer I do violence to Woodstock and to prayer.

Woodstock describes prayer from an immediate point of view. We are *now* invited to a deeper level. Deeper is at the core radical. Immediate is usually peripheral. Woodstock '68 describes prayer immediately, academically, but invites us and frees us to move toward the deeper religious experience of prayer. The statement is one moment in a succession of moments; it is one of many possible perspectives. A perspective is merely a pause, a temporary posture between one movement and the next movement. We appreciate Woodstock because it enables us to see more clearly our spiritual limitation. By this we are enlightened that growth is possible; we are inspired to ask radical (core) questions; we are freed for more profound and interpersonal experience of the Spirit, our Father and Christ His Son. Woodstock is more a gateway through which we embark than a pathway to be tramped over again.

COMMENT

Sister Mary Sullivan, O.P.
Grand Rapids, Michigan

II PERSON AND COMMUNITY

American Sisters deeply desire to take their place within the people of God in the mission of the Church on behalf of human person, for human community—for a better world. We see this investment in the future of the world as a part of our dedication as Christian, celibate women and we know that as American Sisters we have a distinctive contribution to make to the human task of our times.

We stated in all seriousness with foreknowledge of the possible implications: We will be judged by God and by posterity on our persevering willingness to accept and to respond to the call of the Spirit— we will be judged as persons and as communities.

Responding to this call of the Spirit demands that we reject any structure, any attitude in ourselves or in others which would imply that "by our consecration we have become strangers to our fellow men or useless citizens of this earthly city." But "by [our] unswerving and humble loyalty to [our] chosen consecration"—as stated in *Lumen gentium* (ch. 46) we "render to all men generous services of every variety." This is the radical commitment to God and radical commitment to fellow man.

The Woodstock Statement goes on to say that we wish to cooperate with bishops, clergy and the rest of the laity, and with men of good will generally, toward true Christian Community. But we realize that there are situations within the Church where the leadership and responsibility is ours, and we must accept this responsibility and initiate action when we must.

In our General Chapters and Chapters of renewal, American Sisters are envisaging our lives more in terms of person in community. We are relating this vision to the universal struggle of the human person and the community of mankind.

In the Woodstock Statement itself we attempted briefly to state the theological basis of community. We saw religious life as a distinctive way of living the Paschal Mystery, rooted in the mystery of the Trinity as a life rooted in love.

Celibate love, having one heart and soul in Christ, is the bond of religious community. This love is expressed in openness to one another, sensitivity to the needs of others, mutual acceptance of the uniqueness of one another, and mutual availability and concern for the other, a true unity in diversity.

We discussed how both religious community and individual respond to the signs of the times by a blending and a balancing of:

a) Celebration of life, personal and communal. We must be creative and dynamic in our witness to Christ. Our joy in living, our celebration of the liturgy should manifest the reality of our hope in Christ. Coldness and extreme solemnity are aspects of community life which are rejected especially by younger members in religious life.

b) Radical opposition to evil which can only be witnessed by radical commitment to God, and radical commitment to the people of God. Religious communities should be leaders in opposition to social, economic, political and racial injustice whenever and wherever they are able.

c) Reform of attitudes and structures hindering individual and social development. If we are a sign in almost a sacramental sense of the community dimension of the Church, then we must continually evaluate our witness to the Gospel values and adopt proper means for their expression.

d) Professional witness: according to the CMSW Survey American Sisters are better prepared professionally than ever before. With the trend in communities today toward having young women professionally prepared before becoming a part of the community, there must be the constant blending of personal, spiritual, and intellectual witness, of professional witness with personal holiness.

There are some things that I would like to point out about this section on Person and Community. The reflections and recommendations offer not so much new insights as an encouraging witness to one another and to the world. Nor does it presume to express the depth and richness of the mystery of the person and the mystery of community. Nor can it begin to suggest ways of implementing the recommendations in concrete situations within communities, nor can it capture in a single formula the delicate balance and tension between inward- and outward-looking aspects in apostolic community.

Yet in sharing the theme of person and community we have come to realize that the Spirit bestows a wide diversity of gifts, and that celibate Christian Community can have a variety of forms, life styles and accents.

"What must be common to all our efforts is a passion for the dignity, freedom and growth of the human person, a passion for the unity of all men in Christ, passion for the new world founded on truth, directed by justice, realized in freedom, motivated by love and flowering in peace."

COMMENT

Sister Margaret Mary Modde, O.S.F.
Assisi Heights, Rochester, Minnesota

III   INCORPORATION OF NEW MEMBERS INTO THE CONGREGATION

The third section of the Woodstock Statement on Incorporation of New Members into the Congregation is the longest and probably says the least to the reader.

Because of the inadequacy of this section to project the thinking of the Woodstock group it will cause the reader to do some reflective research on several radical questions.

As formation personnel, ours must be a cosmic-like vision which finds its thrust in Vatican II calling for a renewal of religious communities. Basic to this renewal is the formation of each community's members.

Perfectae caritatis says, ". . . the suitable renewal of religious communities depends largely on the training of their new members."

There has been a shift in emphasis from forming a person from the outside, to the providing of an environment in which he can truly develop himself from within. We need to explore the development of forms which will allow the young woman entering a religious community to find herself in her vocation of service; but not only service, for we must also provide forms that are human and flexible enough to allow the mystery of growth in grace to take place.

In the introduction of the statement of "The Incorporation of Candidates into the Congregation," we read that adulthood is manifested by: independence, initiative, ability to handle change, potential to respond to the reality-factors of one's situation, capacity to form true love-relationships, and an inner drive toward growth and freedom. We also read that our society is characterized by rapid change, instability and insecurity.

We are not proposing here that religious communities "get with it," since this is simply the way it is—but we do propose that there is something more creative that religious are able to do in this society besides conform to it, and the creativity of each individual community will determine the kind of person who will be attracted to that community.

The Woodstock Statement continues with: "There must be honest dialogue between the Congregation and the candidates—and the Congregation's part in this honest dialogue is a preliminary evaluation of its own goals and aspirations to see if they are consonant with the goals and aspirations that motivate the people of our time."

We are not presuming here that the goals and aspirations of the people of our time are ideal, or that they are the criteria by which we evaluate our goals.

What is said here is: We need to be doing worthwhile things. We need to have a sense of mission, because young people coming to us want a sense of mission. They want to belong to an organization that has an impact on the world around it, an organization that is sensitive to the world around it, and an organization that can do something about the world around it.

In the section of the Statement which deals with the preparation of the candidate it is stated: "Preparation for life and work in a religious congregation should take place within a context as realistic as possible." By realistic is meant: real-real, practical, functional, immediate. Any kind of artificiality must be rejected. We cannot and must not create special worlds for new members. We already have a world around us, a world that is shouting to us for help.

In *The Church in the Modern World* (n. 62) on "Christian Formation" we read: "May the faithful live in close union with the men of their time [men of *this* world]. Let them strive to understand perfectly their way of thinking and feeling, as expressed in their culture."

Therefore, in order to have our new members develop an acute sensitivity to this world, they must live in an open environment from the beginning, and through the entire formation period.

Religious communities should share their programs and views in order to have a larger vision, but each community must eventually come down to the basics of its own situation, keeping in mind that it must:

1. Prepare the young woman for a life of authentic consecration and service within *everyday* environment;
2. Provide the young woman with the opportunity of continued self-initiated growth toward maturity in order that she be able to make a life-time dedication;
3. Provide the atmosphere in which the young woman may find herself and develop an appreciation of the central values of the congregation and grow in commitment to them;
4. Give ample opportunity to the young women to deepen their Christian life;
5. Provide for professional competence.

The preparation of the new member cannot be considered outside the realm of the role and preparation of the local community, and subsequently the entire community, for we are thrusting upon the shoulders of each individual sister the responsibility of the incorporation of new members. I believe that young women coming to us today will learn to accept the community to the degree that the community accepts her.

The religious congregation through honest dialogue and dependence upon the working of the spirit in each of its members must determine what it sees as religious living. In this context experienced personnel must assist the congregation in their acceptance of the new members, and the new members in their acceptance of the congregation.

In referring to the final means of incorporation, the statement very lightly refers to the evangelical vows: ". . . the vows are one of the traditional forms of complete dedication to a Gospel way of life in the Church." Vows are never explored in the Woodstock Statement; instead the text moves on, and we are encouraged to explore "new forms."

Perhaps this causes us anxiety but this is good, for it will force us to search for new meaning ourselves, for new ways, as the youth of today is searching, and the sisters in our ranks are searching.

The New Norms of Formation, released on February 1, 1969, should give us enthusiasm to investigate and to apply new forms of commitment which will have greater meaning for young women of today.

As formation personnel and major superiors we must scrutinize the signs of the times and relate them to the gospel. We must read between the lines of today's messages. We must interpret the punctuation and fill in the blanks. We must be artists with a sensitive touch, a sharp ear, and a searching eye. The world today is looking for a God beyond technology, and we must know Him. It is expecting a new creation, and must help to create it. The world of today is awaiting a kingdom of peace and we must have been there.

On Adjustment Problems of Black, Mexican-American, Indian, and Rural Candidates to Religious Life

PANEL

Sister M. Alphonsa Spears, O.S.P.
Baltimore, Maryland

I THE BLACK CANDIDATE

The contemporary black sister in the black community has a significant role in the current national contest for racial solidarity, since the present needs of America greatly magnify our role as black religious leaders.

The black nun is an expensive commodity these days. A black community at this time possesses unprecedented bargaining power. The signs of the times of which the Church often speaks has enhanced our role, and accentuated the need for our presence. For the black girl who feels that she has a vocation to the religious life, a radical demand is made upon her. She must ask herself just where she must go to best fulfill her desire to be of service. Will it be to an all-black community or to an integrated community? In what community will she be better able to function as an individual? The greatest danger to the individual in structure-created or community-centered religious life is the loss of individual, creative potential. The process of identifying with the structure, with the community, can produce obviously stylized and stereotyped behavior.

As a member of an all-black community, my first response to the question of where to go would be to say that the black girl should enter the black community. There she will be able to exert influence

among both black and white. There will be no need for her to artificially project herself into the oppressed circumstances of her people.

The black sister in the black community does not need to try to
relate to their problems as many white sisters expend efforts in doing.
We have a built-in system of understanding, since most members of
the black sisterhood have experienced all the humiliations, frustrations,
indignities and rejections that black America experiences. Most of us
have felt the sting of racism prior to and even after entrance into
religion. The black community can open the channels of communication between black and white America, for we represent a power
potential enough to weigh with both. Within our own community we
can speak on racial matters openly, criticize fearlessly, and admonish
sternly without the barrier of color interfering with community.

Members of the black sisterhood have accumulated a total wealth of
experience relative to those specifically affiliated with a predominantly black organization. It has assimilated a whole American tradition, whose attitudes and belief make its members more acutely
aware of both sides of the problem, and opens to them a real opportunity to make both sides complementary. Usually when the sister
of the black community appears before black brothers they listen.
Many place their trust in us because we are black. This says to some
that we have not been brainwashed, as they might suspect of the black
sister in the white community.

On the other hand, the black girl has much to offer the non-black
community. She will have special responsibilities toward the community, a responsibility to enlighten, a responsibility to "tell it like
it is," a responsibility to set her pace, the pace of her people before
the community in a convincing way. She can help the white community better understand the mentality of the black ghetto people,
to appreciate the heritage of the blacks, and to become familiar with
the type of liturgy that appeals to the blacks.

I firmly believe that the white community that accepts the black
candidate should be prepared to relate to that candidate both as an
individual and as a member of a different race, and in most cases, of
a different culture as well. The best way to obtain this end is in treat-
ing each black candidate as a unique human being, as a person. That
is to say, she must be given opportunities to discover her own identity,
because this is her own task.

Somehow the white community must come to grips with what

white culture has done to the entire non-white world, to recognize that other cultures have been looked upon as uncivilized, instead of as simply being different. This is something deeply rooted in our society; it is not a surface thing. In order to help the black girl maintain her cultural differences the white community might allow her to study her own culture, to continue to participate in black activities, to procure black music and books by black writers for her enjoyment as well as the enjoyment and enrichment of the other members of the community. There is need today to expose the whole community to black culture; there is a need to expose the whole world to the riches it contains.

The white community that accepts the black candidate is faced with the need for various adjustments on both sides, that of the candidate and that of the community. Just how this adjustment is made depends a great deal on the candidate's personality and on the stance of the community. If the candidate is asked to be a religious first and a black person secondly, then she is being asked to live a lie, to deny what is culturally hers, to forfeit her birthright. In a sense she is asked to sell her soul. Somehow, and it is very difficult at this time to say just how, we must guard against mere co-existence. The black sister must be accepted as a total member of the community, not as a mere symbolic figure.

The question before us now, faced by every religious community today, is how can we set up effective vocation programs to contact potential black vocations. For many communities this will simply mean opening their doors to the black applicant.

Communities must strip themselves of paternalism, promote the relevance of the Church in a black community, and take definite steps toward making the Church meaningful in the black communities. To these decisions communities must join prayer. Let us all pray God to change hearts, to enlighten minds, and let us pray with faith. I am sure that since the Lord said, "Faith can move mountains," He will certainly enable us to move the mountains of mistrust and injustice that handicap us all. May this panel be extremely fruitful in giving us a vision, in giving us courage, because God has assuredly given us a destiny.

II THE BLACK CANDIDATE

Sister Anna, S.B.S.
Cornwell Heights, Pennsylvania

Since I am a black sister from a white community, I will do my best to speak for those few who are in similar circumstances, or for those who are aspiring to enter a white community. The possibility of black and white girls living together in community life has sometimes been questioned. Why should a black aspirant wish to live this type of vocation? Should not the aspirant be encouraged to go to an all-black community?

It would seem, however, that if the apostolic work of a white congregation is totally or partially among blacks, that congregation should make an honest effort to have black religious as an integral part of the community. The need to dispel or change the idea among blacks that Catholicism is a white man's religion, and that the Church is a white racist society impels religious to encourage black vocations.

Man can better identify with that society which tries to identify with him. For the success of the apostolate among them, black people must see black priests and sisters coming to them, must get to know them as friends.

Whites who attempt to teach the black man how to love God and his fellowmen, yet refuse themselves to accept black candidates, to truly accept them, shout by their actions if not by their words, the pharisaical attitude denounced by Christ, "Don't do as I do, do as I say."

Blacks in some areas are now saying, "We want only black teachers for our black children." The dearth of black vocations makes this impossible at the present time. A black religious living in a white community, however, can help to express the needs and thinking of her people to the members of her community, and thus be a means by which the Order can show that it is sympathetic to the black cause.

Certainly black vocations should not be encouraged for the mere purpose of pacifying the public, or of improving the community's self image. The religious community is at the service of the Church. If an integrated religious family is to serve the Church authentically, responding to the needs of the people in a more effective manner, then black girls must be invited to join the community so that they can witness to Christ among the people. Let black girls follow the guidance of the Holy Spirit, but white communities must make it possible for them to do so.

Those who are really awake to the movement of the Holy Spirit today are aware of the need to know new trends in black thinking. Those communities that are accepting black candidates, or are planning to do so in the future should reevaluate their ideas and attitudes about blacks, should read widely in books which help to explain the black movement, and should take advantage of courses in cultural anthropology. Such courses and books can help to dispel strange notions that exist about black people that are not always voiced. Certainly those communities accepting black candidates should carefully evaluate the racial attitudes of those in charge of formation.

There is need for self-evaluation regarding true Christianity within the religious community. Why should a girl be encouraged to enter a community where she will be demeaned because of her race and culture? Some house cleaning may need to be done before the step is taken that will permit embracing the black man as a true brother.

Black candidates, on the other hand, must understand that those with whom they are going to live are frail human beings, and they must not be shocked by prejudicial attitudes which have not yet been eradicated, even in religious lives.

Courses of study in anthropology and sociology will help communities understand and adjust to various differences whether racial, ethnic or socio-economic in each of their candidates, whether black or white.

William Osborne's *The Segregated Covenant* (New York: Herder and Herder, 1967) gives an excellent survey and graphic picture of the origin of segregated religious institutions in the United States. Books like this will help communities receiving the black candidate, and especially those in charge of formation, to understand the basic differences between aspirants from the South and those from the North. Myrdal's *American Dilemma* (New York: Harper, 1944) and Franklin Fraizier's *Negro Church in America* (New York: Schocken Books, 1964) help one to understand differences in cultures. In a brief paper such as this it would be impossible to go into these differences at length.

Now what can be said about the oversensitive black aspirant? In the case of the candidate who gets so emotionally defensive about her blackness that she attributes *every* correction she receives to the fact that she is black rather than that she is wrong, it is obvious she has not achieved the type of maturity which is integral and which can stand the test of correction on individual and personal performance. She is probably not quite ready for religious life, and needs help in growing up. This is frequently a problem for the psychologist. However, if in some instances the candidate's correction does spring from prejudicial motives, certainly this type of action should be recognized and changed on the part of those administering the correction.

In general, young black girls are like other vivacious, eager candidates. They do not wish either to be catered to or treated harshly. They do not wish to be shown off as a prize package to certain community visitors, or excluded on other occasions lest their blackness offend some official dignitary.

There is a widespread concern about the lack of vocations, and how to set up effective vocational programs. One means to attract black vocations in a closer contact with black people. Religious should live among black people, not drive into the inner city apostolate from ultra-comfortable convents. Rather, after the example of Christ, they should live among those to whom the apostolate is directed. A sincere manifestation of a sympathetic attitude toward the black community and its own distinctive heritage is a fruitful means to draw black vocations.

We know that prayer and sacrifice accomplish more than mere words. However, with God's help may these few words give impetus to the necessary sacrifices, so that our black sisters may share the task of tending the Lord's vineyard.

Suggested Questions For Preparing A Community Panel On This Subject:
1. Should we encourage black girls to enter all-white communities or advise them to enter black communities? Why or why not?
2. What type of orientation, if any, should we give the sisters receiving the black girl? What should we give the candidate?
3. Are there cultural differences between white and black people? How can we help the black candidate maintain these differences and be proud of them?
4. How can we help a black candidate who feels that every correction she gets is because she is black rather than because she is wrong?
5. Is there a difference between the southern black and the northern black?

6. There are very few black sisters in the U.S. How can we set up effective vocation programs and contact potential black vocations?

III THE MEXICAN-AMERICAN CANDIDATE

Sister M. Floretta, M.C.D.P.
San Antonio, Texas

I belong to the Missionary Catechists of Divine Providence, an all Mexican-American community founded by the Divine Providence Sisters of San Antonio. I would like to open my talk with an incident that happened to me when I was planning to enter the convent. I went to the Incarnate Word sisters until the eighth grade. (I say this in all charity because until this incident I had never realized there was a difference between Mexican-Americans and Anglo-Americans, or that some communities were all Mexican-American and others were integrated.) One of the Incarnate Word sisters who had taught me asked me why I was entering this particular community. I said, "Because I like the work they do."

Then she said, "Why don't you come and visit our convent? We have big buildings, while your group is small." Then she asked me again, "Well, why do you want to go there?"

I said, "I would like to do their work. That's what interests me."

She answered, "You know they are all Mexican-Americans."

I replied, "Well, what's the difference? I like to do that type of work." After that I did enter the Missionary Catechists, not because they were all Mexican-Americans, but because I wanted to be involved in the type of religious education work which the sisters do.

To speak now of what the Mexican-American feels in the community, I will speak first of the Mexican-American. America is the melting pot of the world with many races and nationalities. Because of this it is difficult for many to realize that there is still prejudice, that Americans find it difficult to understand each other, even American religious.

I feel that the problems of adjustment of candidates to our community should be few, since they all grow up as Americans. Today there are not so many obvious differences between families of Anglo- and Mexican-Americans. We go to the same public schools; we follow the same routines, we are actually involved in society. However, there is a difference in the family structure. The Mexican family is more united; the parents like to form their children in a stricter manner; they do not allow them as much freedom as parents of Anglo-American boys and girls.

However, as we see society changing, even this is changing within the Mexican-American families. Today many Mexican-American girls have the same freedom that Anglo-American girls have. By the time they enter the convent as high school graduates they are almost the same as the Anglo-American girl except in their cultural background.

We have inherited from our parents Mexican customs that they have inherited from their parents. This common culture is what makes it easier for us, an exclusively Mexican-American community. We are all the same; we have the same ideals and the same goals. Of course, we have problems. We all come from different families, but our problems are more the adjustment to different personalities rather than to different cultures.

Now I should like to speak of the integrated community. Initially, we did have Anglo-American superiors and directors of formation from the Sisters of Divine Providence. There were problems, but we have learned a lot.

The question we must ask ourselves is: who is to make the adjustment? Is it to be the Mexican-American, just because she is one of the so-called minority groups? Yet, who are the minority groups, who are the ethnic groups? We cannot say that one is better than the other. We were all born in the United States. We are all American citizens. What is the difference? Each has a different culture, a different heritage. The thing to remember is not that one must adjust to the other, but that there should be a mutual understanding. I must adjust to any sister that I meet, whether she is black, Indian, or white, because I must meet her as a person. It is because of her unique quality that I accept her, not because of her race or heritage.

We must really learn the culture of each race; superiors and directors of formation are especially responsible here. If they know and understand each particular race and the particular culture of each individual, they will be able to help the sister as well as enable other sisters to accept her. It is through this mutual sharing that we learn.

The Mexican-American is very sensitive, very proud and often very stubborn. All men have these tendencies, but they are more pronounced in the Mexican-American. Sometimes a correction is given that will be attributed to prejudice. However, if the directress really understands Mexican culture, she will be able to handle this situation, and there will be no tension or misunderstanding, and the candidate will be helped to self-growth.

We must recognize the presence of prejudice toward other races even among the sisters themselves. We speak here, and yet many of us will not be able to overcome this prejudice in spite of the fact that we have heard the problem stated. When we come to a group meeting such as this we are sometimes more able to accept a sister from another community than the one in our own. This is where the problem really lies. If we are really sincere we will try to accept each other as Christ did.

We are all mixed in this melting pot that is America. Just because my English is broken and I sometimes speak with an accent, should not make so much difference to anyone. If we are Christian, we try to share with each other, and create a better religious life for everybody.

Suggested Questions for Preparing a Community Panel On This Subject:
1. What type of cultural changes must a Mexican-American candidate expect when she enters an Anglo-American community?
2. What can the community do to make these adjustments easier?
3. Should we encourage Mexican-American candidates to enter congregations made up only of Mexican-Americans or should we encourage them to enter Anglo-American congregations? Why or why not?
4. Would you advise a period of special orientation for Mexican-American girls entering an Anglo-American congregation. What should it consist of?
5. What obstacles does the Mexican-American candidate face: from her parents, from society, from the community?
6. What type of vocation-promotion program can we set up to contact the Mexican-American candidate?

IV THE INDIAN CANDIDATE

Sister M. Consolata, S.B.S.
Cornwell Heights, Pennsylvania

It might be wise to acquaint you briefly with the general background of the American Indian. I am sure that you are all aware of the differences between the many tribes—from their mythical origins to languages, traditional practices such as healing ceremonies, dances, whether of a more solemn or merely of a social nature; the varied range of celebrations such as the joyful celebration of a deer hunt which honors the hunter with a Pueblo deer dinner, or the Apache Indian wake, with its week-long preparation for the final night before the body is finally laid to rest. Although there are these differences, there are some attitudes and values which are common to almost all tribes. Some of these are their generosity, sharing, respect for individual freedom, adjustment to nature, deep reverence for the old, love of nature and the right use of it. These and more are common elements possessed in a greater or lesser degree within the various tribes.

With this background, though brief, let us consider the average young Indian adult of today. She comes from a people who are struggling, struggling to hold on to all that which is so meaningful to their culture, and that which makes them who they are. Yet they are caught up in the fast pace which marks the average American. The young Indian comes from a people striving for the acquisition of independence, in their own family, in their community, their tribe; but before her people can realize independence they must have a reservoir of trained and professional people. We American Indians do not yet have sufficient numbers to fulfill the professional needs of our communities and institutions. The young Indian has not been encouraged by her parents to prepare herself intellectually for the future. There has not been in her home the atmosphere of "desire to learn." Formal education has not been a necessity on the reservations, and has yet to be recognized and realized.

It is a rare, rare occasion for the young Indian to see an Indian doctor, teacher, lawyer, sister, priest. Where can she get her inspiration? A vocation is a gift of God, a divine call, but I believe that it is begun, nurtured and sustained in a family.

It is a deeply rooted custom among the Indian that one return to the place where one's life began, to finish life and be buried there. This custom has been instilled, unconsciously, in the young Indian, and Indian parents believe that achievement in education is a sure sign that there will be a permanent separation from the homeland. How much more then, do they fear a religious vocation. It may breed resentment in a family. The young adult realizes the strong hold this value has on her—that desire to prolong the heritage of a proud people. On the other hand, there is that growing desire for human happiness which every non-Indian values so highly, for some achievement, some success.

A quality which the young Indian girl has yet to acquire is self-motivation. After beginning some training, education, or profession, she quickly gives up; she lacks that "stick-to-it-iveness" which is so necessary to accomplish anything. Unlike her non-Indian neighbors she is not future-oriented; she lives on a day-to-day basis. Immediate gratification is a rule rather than the delaying of gratification for the future. Then there is the authoritarianism in the formation of the religious which conflicts with the Indian way of life, the Indian's use of individual freedom. Indian children have the freedom to move, act, and take responsibility for themselves. The average parent seems to be unaware that in today's complex society children are not prepared for or capable of making decisions. In the attainment of these qualities so necessary in religious life, the Indian will need much guidance and counseling.

Before we can promote vocations among the Indian, the Indians themselves have to realize that they must take their place in society and fill the common positions in the dominant culture. I believe that the establishment of the faith is a real necessity for the budding forth of religious vocations. I also believe that before the whisperings of the Holy Spirit can be heard there must be instilled in the Indian a sensitivity to His promptings.

V THE RURAL CANDIDATE

Sister M. Donald, C.S.A.
Sister M. Josephine, C.S.A.
Fond du Lac, Wisconsin

Bernard Häring once said that we as religious in communities must beware in our screening process, of admitting only persons with the same attitudes and outlooks of those doing the screening.

A look at the adjustment problems of the rural versus the city candidate admits of possibility for variation of personality, although that is not a direct purpose of these comments.

My stress of the rural adjustment problems are observations culled from three sources:

1. Pointed articles about rural versus urban girls are rare. Usually one finds, of course, the same human needs, emotional drives, social pulls, physical patterns and life visions. The difference lies in their degree;
2. Eight years of close contact in formation work, counseling of high school girls, and direct current work with adolescents gives me some insight into this area;
3. It has been my privilege to attend many vocation-oriented meetings, conferences and workshops. I have been active in diocesan planning and participation in vocation endeavors.

We cannot come up with a purely rural type or a purely urban type. The focus on the rural brings out many advantages, and a few disadvantages that affect her adjustment. We may, however, say that rural-ness and urban-ness complement one another. There is not time to comment directly on the urban girl, especially since she is not the object of this talk.

The rural girl has many outstanding characteristics:

1. A sturdy attitude towards work, a rugged, thorough endurance that usually sees a job to the finish;
2. A wholesome outlook on lesser bodily ailments that make the city

girl run for aspirin or band-aids. Scratches, bumps, cramps and headaches are not considered important enough for attention;

3. A beautiful thirst for prayer and the transcendent, possibly because of a closely-knit family background based on a sincere dependence on God for livelihood;

4. The knowledge that she is *needed* in her family gives the rural girl a distinct advantage over her city counterpart. Time is valuable to her, and she generally uses it to good advantage;

5. A seriousness about studies—a by-product of an understanding of the work behind the money paid out for her education.

These are all plus factors. She has other characteristics we can call her minus factors. Chief among them are:

1. Low self-concept often a result of her misinformed idea that the rural is below the urban on the ladder of importance. As a result, she is often shy and non-aggressive;

2. Frequently she shows an inability to relate to people in groups, because of past, too-confined interest patterns;

3. Seldom does she have the opportunity to meet or befriend sisters. The adjustments she must make, then, in religious life lie in the areas of her characteristics.

Socially, she will need to broaden her interests, to let herself out for relationships with other people outside her family circle or immediate friends.

She can expect to suffer deeply from homesickness for a time, and she will probably have a greater struggle than most in becoming autonomous in non-rural surroundings or circumstances.

She may experience frustration because she is so sensitive to others, sees their needs and wants to help them, but lacks the daring to do what she really wants to do!

Concerning the rural candidate we need to remember that praise will go a long, long way to build and support a sometimes weak self-confidence. Formal discussions and experiences about the techniques of relating socially are often most appreciated by her. Assisting her to find her "thing" (as teenagers say) will move her quickly towards a higher self-concept, *i.e.*, music, art, drama, a hobby, involvement in volunteer programs with other people. Suggesting good enriching reading with worldwide view will open possibilities for her for broader views and discussions.

Often, modern girls long for a word or gesture of approval from the adult authority figures, parents or superiors. People are too busy to think about praising and patting backs. More of it would bring out the hidden beauty.

To reach the rural candidate many avenues are wide open because of her open attitude to the sublime. Contacts with religious are for her a unique experience. It takes only a quick evaluation of persons available and willing to assist, and a workable program to reach the non-urban girl.

One approach that was successful, if this can be determined by interest and response, is the three-fold approach in vocation work which aims at reaching:

1. Adults, with the objective of educating parents to the humanity of the sisters, and to current trends in religious life and renewal. A panel of priest, brother, sister and married couple discusses frankly personal feelings towards current issues;
2. High school students, with the objective of preparing the student for a sound, objective decision towards a life style;
3. T.E.C. or Teens Encounter Christ is geared toward building Christian leaders through authentic self-concept in relation to God and others;
4. Probe—a type of recollection-discussion evening with panel as above to give time to stop and think through for awhile, self-concept and Christianity;
5. Probe, as above, geared to grade school mentality;
6. Torch, a club indirectly educating toward life decision, interested in all vocations and geared to provide much needed opportunities for children outside the teacher-student relationship with sisters.

Contemporary Theology and Sisters' Prayer Life

REV. THOMAS DUBAY, S.M.
Russell College, Burlingame, California

Contemporary theology is exciting theology. It is rich, diversified, moving. It presents new approaches and new emphases. Some of these approaches and emphases are obviously relevant to the developing prayer life of religious women. We shall here touch upon six of these emphases together with their implications for contemplative and liturgical communion with the Lord.

Area I: *Man as Transcendental*

Man is an incarnated thirst. He thirsts, but not as a mere animal does, that is, for particulars. He thirsts for a beyond, insatiably, without end, without resting. The more a man is alive, the more he thirsts. The intellectually keen person is forever curious, always asking questions, unceasingly reading a new book or discussing an old problem. The artist never finds himself filled with created beauties. The miser never amasses a large enough fortune. The hedonist forever seeks new and exotic foods, drinks, sexual encounters. The saint unceasingly pursues God, his sole universal good. Like parched earth, dry, lifeless, without water, he seeks his God. Man, says contemporary theology, is a dynamism pointed to the beyond. As incarnated spirit he bursts through the boundaries of the concrete order in his incessant hunger for the Absolute. The psalmist immortalized this thrust to the transcendent Beyond when he admonished himself: in God alone be at rest, my soul.

What conclusions may we draw for a sister's prayer life from this theological emphasis? 1.) Simply as a human being, even aside from her being a religious, she must have a deep inner communion with God. Nothing else will rest her, nothing: not work, not success, not clothes, not freedom, not even human love. "In God alone be at rest, my soul." 2.) As a woman she cannot make it in life without a profound, exclusive, intimate love. Without this love she may survive, but she will not blossom fully as a woman. If in her vows she gives up a hoped-for love in marriage, where will she achieve this deep, exclusive love if not in her prayer communion with her indwelling Beloved? A sister who thinks she is a religious primarily for the external apostolate not only does not understand theology—she does not understand her femininity. 3.) If man as spirit is an incarnated thirst dynamically and necessarily pointed to the Absolute, it follows that he is first of all a pursuer of Beauty and only secondarily a worker-producer. Or as Vatican II would have it, in the Church "action is directed and subordinated to contemplation." (Constitution on the Sacred Liturgy, no. 2) In her efforts to solve the time pressure problem a sister must put prayer first in her value system. She may not allow a second thing to squeeze out or suffocate a first thing. Her solution, given life as it is, will have to be radical. But the theology behind it is also radical. What is the primary reason you sisters are in a diocese? Religious "foster these objectives [of building up the Mystical Body] *primarily* by means of *prayer*, works of *penance*, and the *example* of their own life." (Decree on Bishops' Pastoral Office, no. 33.) External apostolate is mentioned later, not among the primary means. Is this possibly just the opposite of what some of us suppose in our day-to-day routine? Do you think of yourself in the Church first of all as a woman of prayer, a worker of penance, a giver of saintly example? This view is admittedly radical.

Area II: *Ecclesial Indwelling*

Yahweh dynamically present among His people was the whole atmosphere of the Old Testament. He was to them a God who was there, in their midst, acting, speaking, enlightening, rebuking, comforting, working marvels. The Holy Spirit dynamically present in the new people of God, the Church, is the omnipresent atmosphere of the new theology. He is also present in an impelling way, moving, vivifying, unifying, renewing, teaching. He is the giver of charisms, the giver of love. The Church as Spirited-Communion is perhaps the central doctrinal theme of Vatican II.

What is the relevance of the indwelling Spirit for your prayer life and mine? The relevance is so crushingly obvious that I hesitate to spell it out. Sacred Scripture presents the indwelling of the Spirit (and of the Father and the Son) as a tissue of intersubjective relationships: mutual knowing, loving, possessing, delighting.[1] These same inter-personal relationships are, of course, what contemplative prayer is all about. Personal presence demands communion. The indwelling presence demands communion, and essentially demands it. This is why the Council could assign to contemplation a place at the very core of ecclesial reality: "It is of the *essence* of the Church that she be both . . . eager to act and yet devoted to contemplation." (Const. on the Sacred Liturgy, no. 2) I am eager to work, all right. No problem here. But am I *devoted* to contemplation? . . . Are you? Are your young sisters? The consecrated virgin stands among the people of God, these living stones in the Temple-Church, as one who is emi-nently concerned with "the things of the Lord," she who is free from care that she may pray without distraction.[2] The consecrated virgin is an ecclesial woman, and an ecclesial woman is not exactly the same reality as a career woman.

Area III: *Charismatic Freedom*

"Where the Spirit of the Lord is, there is freedom." [3] It is no acci-dent that the same modern theology which stresses the ecclesial in-dwelling also stresses the Spirit-originated freedom enjoyed by the sons of God. To see more clearly the relationship between this new liberty and our prayer life we shall first review briefly the nature of the former.

The freedom of the Christified man supposes our native psycho-logical power of self-determination and goes far beyond it. Spirit-originated freedom basically means that a man is so enlightened and moved by the indwelling Spirit that he spontaneously carries out the written law of Christ. He is free of external coercion, penalty, threat. The shackles of sin, blindness, absurdity fall from his person. Freely, gently moved by the perfect inner law, the in-abiding God, this man is opened to goodness, light, beauty, to the completion of his human-ness. He wants what he does, really desires it. The God within is effecting the will, and the execution.[4] He is man led by the Spirit, a son of God.[5] He is sometimes a man so sensitive to this abiding Spirit that he is a charismatic wonder-worker. "Ordinarily," remarks

Vatican II, "God desires to manifest His *wonders* through those who have been made particularly docile to the impulse and guidance of the Holy Spirit." [6] Wonders of freedom, nothing less.

Because contemplation is a gift of the Spirit before it is an activity of a man, the more sensitive this man is to the divine impulse the more profound will his contemplation be. And conversely, the deeper his prayer is, the more he is moved by the Spirit, the more he is opened and liberated. Freedom and contemplation fit hand in glove. Not only does theology teach this truth. Concrete life illustrates it. The profoundly prayerful man is remarkably free of fear, whether it be the fear of human respect or external law. He knows neither the degrading slavery of a sinful habit nor the depressing burden of an icy, God-absent universe. He literally rejoices in the Lord always, and enjoys a peace that surpasses understanding.[7] His sensitivity to the Spirit has Christified him.

Yet this delightful, liberating contemplation demands a price. We would lack honesty were we to suggest otherwise—we would likewise be lacking in fidelity to the gospel. A man is not free merely by wishing to be free, nor is he docile to the Divine Initiator simply by being attracted to the idea. This is the point at which gospel asceticism enters the picture. If a religious finds contemplation meaningless, she may begin her critique not with contemplation but with an investigation into the totality of her living the gospel, into her own detachment, penance, mortification. Is she reading the self-denial texts as well as the joy texts? Is she unwittingly selective? If she is, she will be neither free nor contemplative. New Testament examples literally abound. We shall note two only. What is one reason religious may not reach a profound prayer life, a profound response to the word of God sown in their hearts? Listen to the divine diagnosis: "As for the part that fell into thorns, this is people who have heard, but as they go on their way they are choked by the worries and riches and pleasures of life and do not reach maturity." [8] There is no condemnation here of cares or wealth or pleasure. There is question of suffocation. Good things can suffocate. Both asceticism and involvement are necessary for growth. And so is an inner detachment. Apostolic, involved Paul could tie the incarnational in with the eschatological: "Since you have been brought back to true life with Christ, you must look for the things that are in heaven, where Christ is . . . Let your thoughts be on heavenly things, not on the things that are on the earth." [9] This is one of the prices of freedom.

Our new emphasis on Spirit-originated liberty implies, finally, that the sister be mature enough to *want* a deep contemplative communion with her Beloved. Our reduction of prayer structures requires as a corollary that we so grow in sensitivity to the Holy Spirit that we allow Him to lead us to desire and to attain what the structures were meant to achieve. Because a legal morality is minimal, and a love morality maximal, the Spirit who pours love into our hearts will lead us beyond what the mere external law could require. We are free not in order to do less but to do more. The virgin is free from care in order to be utterly available to the Lord.

Area IV: *Experience of God*

Even though many of us may feel a nameless ambivalence regarding the whole question of experiencing divine reality, we cannot deny that the question lies in the forefront of modern man's mind. Theologians speak about an awareness of grace-realities, and Vatican II assumed an experience of God both in the contemplation of private prayer, and in the midst of the liturgical celebration.[10] The ancient Hebrew sang about tasting and seeing how good the Lord is and about growing radiant with joy through an encounter with Him.[11] The current occupation with psychedelically induced awarenesses and oriental mysticism seems to indicate a similar interest. So likewise does the rapid spread of pentecostalism and its baptism of the Spirit and the experience of Jesus.

What do these phenomena say to us about the meaningfulness of prayer for the modern sister? I hear a message that sounds very much like the heart of being human. I hear the idea that man is not made to be a functionary but to be plunged into the heart of God. I conclude that your prayer life and mine are meant to develop into a fullness that eye has not seen nor ear heard, a fullness in which we really taste and see how sweet the Lord is. I conclude that the ecstatic language of a Bernard of Clairvaux, a Teresa of Avila, a John of the Cross, trying to describe the indescribable is to be taken seriously and soberly, not as mere pious exaggerations of bygone ages. I conclude that we ought not to dilute the ecstatic language of the psalter either, that all this is meant for you and me.

But you know that the experience of God of which we are speaking is not had for nothing; God is not to be had cheap. We may need new prayer forms but they will not render obsolete our human need for solitudes with the Father. Christ is forever valid. And Christ habitually spent long hours, even whole nights, at prayer. Mark and Luke have a whole series of texts relating how He would repeatedly integrate into His apostolic work solitudes for communion with his Father. In one of these texts Luke is able to summarize all the others: "He would *always* go off to some place where He could be alone and pray." [12] Do you always go off to some place where you can be alone and pray? Are you forming your young sisters to union with this kind of Christ?

Area V: *Pilgrim Poverty*

We hesitate to speak of poverty and prayer because of the magnitude of the problem. A pat solution to our poverty problems (for example, dropping the vow in favor of a vow of community) can perhaps be explained in a few words. Grappling with the real issues would take us much longer and then we would have merely touched the surface. We shall have to be content with a few hints. The first hint we know well: the New Testament is full of the praise of voluntary poverty, both of fact and of spirit. The second hint: Vatican II is replete with the same praise. The third hint: most of us American religious are not poor. The fourth hint: yet both contemporary theology and Vatican II speak eloquently of the pilgrim Church following in the footsteps of the poor Christ. Our last hint: Christ was not poor by accident but by choice. There is a connection between leaving all things and having Him fully.[13]

What is the point of poverty for prayer? The Council put the idea perfectly: "Human freedom is often crippled when a man falls into extreme poverty, just as it withers when he indulges in too many of life's comforts and imprisons himself in a kind of splendid isolation." [14] Yes, destitution kills humanness. Luxury suffocates it. You and I are not destitute, but we may be more or less smothered in a splendid isolation. One must be free to contemplate. The pilgrim Church is pointed to the *eschaton*. She is on a sacred journey. She travels lightly. Says Paul, "We brought nothing into the world, and we can take nothing out of it; but as long as we have food and clothing, let us be content with that." [15] Voluntary poverty provides freedom; profound contemplation flourishes in it.

Area VI: *Biblical Renewal*

The soul of the new theology is scriptural. The basic norm for the rejuvenation of the religious life is Christ in the gospel. The spark of prayer communion with our indwelling Beloved is the word of God. The virgin is a woman of the word, yes, and of the Word . . . and this for several reasons. First, she is a woman of faith. The virgin's life grows out of faith, is supported by faith, is enlightened by faith. She is a sign before the world of the fulfillment of faith. The virgin is blessed because she has believed. Second, she is an ecclesial woman. She stands in the midst of God's people as concerned wholly with the affairs of the Lord. At work and at prayer she is the feminine minister of the word. Third, as concerned with the word she is a fruitful mother. Just as St. Paul begot his Corinthians by the Gospel,[16] so does the consecrated woman give new birth to men through the same good news. She is so full of the word that she necessarily communicates it to others. She has come as mother that men may have life and have it to the full. Fourth, her prayer is richly fed by Sacred Scripture. Again as an ecclesial woman she joins her fellows in the pilgrim Church and sees her God in the sacred pages. This divine labor, this acting, moving, driving word works contemplation in her. If "for God to speak is to do," [17] the divine message is fecundating her being to faith and love. It is living, acting, cutting, piercing like a two-edged sword.[18] Fifth, the virgin's purity purifies her to a complete receptivity to the word. If, as Paul reminds us, the sensual man cannot understand the things of the Spirit, if it is nonsense to him precisely because he is sensual, the virgin is especially attuned to the Spirit . . . to receive and grasp and grow. Lastly, the religious woman responds to the word by being eminently the contemplatrix in the Church. She is Mary drinking in Christ at the feet of Christ. She must work, of course. But she first of all pursues the great "one thing." She seeks with the psalmist as the one thing to dwell in the house of the Lord all the days of her life, to gaze on the loveliness of the Lord.

ACADEMIC PREPARATION

We may now turn our attention to our second task, academic formation in prayer. In the more simple days of past centuries a less complex education for the religious life was adequate. It is probably still adequate for more simple people today. But for many of today's religious a thorough academic preparation for a life of prayer is indispensable. Though we have greatly improved other areas of sister formation, we have scarcely scratched the surface of this one. I would venture to guess that the majority of formation personnel would be the first to admit not only that their instructional programs in contemplation are inadequate, but also that they themselves do not know what an adequate program would be. I shall be rash enough to suggest to you what I think a thorough formation in prayer would include. I will speak in terms of units and approximate number of formal experience hours (academic and otherwise) each unit might contain.

Unit 1: *Psychology and Philosophy of Inter-subjective Relationships*
(20–25 hours)

Using the riches both of perennial philosophy and contemporary personalism and existentialism, this unit would investigate deeply what knowledge, love, delight, and possession really are. On a merely human level it would discover just what man-and-man intersubjective relationships imply. Is not prayer precisely man-to-God intersubjectivity of the most profound type?

Unit 2: *Old Testament Prayer Themes*
(5 or 10 seminar hours preceded by student research.)

A careful study of the psalter alone yields 12 or 15 beautifully expressed prayer themes, e.g. yearning for Yahweh, experience of Him, wondering at Him, delight in the Lord, the tender, loving kindness of Yahweh, continual prayer. To find, compare, interrelate, and apply the many texts illustrating each theme yields a touchingly beautiful and concrete picture of what man's communion with his God really means. Experience shows that young women are powerfully attracted by this unit.

Unit 3: *Indwelling Mystery of the New Testament*
(10–15 hours)

Contemplation is nothing other than an intimate communion with one's indwelling Beloved. This unit would present the New Testament revelation in the light of Units 1 and 2. It would be both Biblical and speculative, and practical.

Unit 4: *Systematic Study of Contemplation*
(25–30 hours)

This unit would deal both speculatively and experimentally with what contemplation is, with various approaches to prayer for beginners, with an experimental and detailed description of how communion with God usually develops, with the inner relationships between liturgy and contemplation, with the impediments to growth. It would take up sundry problems: silence, distractions, aridity, spiritual direction integrating action and contemplation. This unit should be heavily illustrated with examples from Units 1 and 2.

Unit 5: *Advanced Reading Seminar for Junior Professed*
(50–60 hours of seminar sessions)

This final stage of our formal academic preparation for contemplative prayer consists of reading ten books, both classical and contemporary, together with seminar discussion sessions for one two-hour period each week. During this current scholastic year I am experimenting with this approach in three seminar groups of ten or eleven sisters each. Among the books we are reading are:

Joseph Pieper, *Leisure, Basis of Culture*
Happiness and Contemplation
Thomas Merton, *Mystics and Zen Masters* (selected chapters)
Gregory of Nyssa, *On Virginity, From Glory to Glory* (Excerpts)
Karl Rahner, *On Prayer*
Teresa of Avila, *Interior Castle*
John of the Cross, *Dark Night of the Soul*
Spiritual Canticle

In addition to the reading and seminar sessions, each student is assigned a research paper which, when finished, she duplicates and distributes to each student in all three groups. She defends her paper in seminar session and in the light of the other two papers on the same subject. The topics of research are meant to complete and deepen understanding of contemplation. Those assigned for this year include the following:

1. Contemplation and liturgy: interrelations
2. Contemplation and purification in Teilhard de Chardin
3. God as man's consummating fruition
4. Experimental traits of infused contemplation

5. Divine transcendence in Rahner, and infused contemplation
6. Solitude with God: a biblical study
7. Yoga and prayer
8. Virginity and contemplation in the Catholic tradition
9. Contemplation of faith and vision.

So much for our suggested program. One may object—and with no little plausibility—that so extensive a study is well and good in theory but practically impossible in fact. Who would possess the competencies to teach these courses effectively, and where would the time be found for the sheer number of class hours, not to mention study opportunity? One can sympathize with these difficulties. Yet we may make several observations in return. Granted, this program does call for much time and talent. But so do any number of other important human endeavors. Do we religious really believe what Scripture and Vatican II say about the primacy of a contemplative communion with the Lord? Is our belief merely token or is it also practical? Should not this belief surface obviously in our sister formation programs?

We may note likewise that parts of this program could be executed in an interdisciplinary manner. Unit one on intersubjectivity could be taught by a person in philosophy, unit two by a biblicist, and unit three by a theologian. If such be done, the several instructors should, of course, plan and work together.

A final observation regarding our object: this program would carry along with it a number of valuable by-products. Unit one would strengthen the sister's grasp on the nature of community and ordinary human interpersonal relationships. Unit two would present a new facet to the sister's knowledge of Yahweh and the ancient Hebrew's relations with Him. Unit three would cast new light in many areas of theology: incarnation, grace, Church, the beatific vision, risen body. The reading seminar, unit five, would help to broaden the young religious in several areas: leisure, oriental contemplation, patristic literature, Spanish poetry. The research papers would serve this same function in still other areas: liturgy, transcendental theology, virginity, yoga, Teilhard de Chardin.

Atmosphere of Prayer

Our final task is brief, though its aim is crucial. We wish to say a word about an atmosphere for prayer. Neither new theology nor improved instruction is enough. Ordinary people need reasonably propitious surroundings if they are to grow. Just as a candidate for a doctoral degree in physics or biology will not master his field unless he makes up his mind to spend hours and days in silent study as well as in fruitful classroom communication, so also does the Christian, any Christian, have to learn how to combine communion with men with a solitude before God. We cannot live the continual prayer theme of both testaments, we cannot relive the great and frequent solitudes of Jesus with his Father, unless we have the atmosphere of quiet in which to do it. As spirit man is contemplative. As incarnated he is conditioned by the concrete, existential, here-and-now situation. Prayer on earth does not happen in an aseptic, pure, angelic haven. Prayer does not just happen. It must be prepared for. We prepare for it by an atmosphere of reverence and silence, by a warm love and trust among the sisters, by the strength issuing from mutual, prayerful example. Sister Formation personnel should be prayerful women before they are anything else.

Contemporary theology is biblically inspired. The sister is a woman of the word. Whether or not she shall be a prayerful woman can be ascertained by her honest response to some scriptural questions:

Am I seriously in a hot pursuit of the Lord, not a mediocre moving, but an ardent running? "As the doe longs for running streams, so longs my soul for you, my God. My soul thirsts for God, the God of life." Can I say this honestly?

Am I so given to prayerfulness that I would consider it normal to say, "Happy those who live in Your house and can praise You all the day long"?

Is my life so gravitated toward God that I can make my own the absolute admonition of the psalmist: "Rest in God alone, my soul"?

Am I reliving the prayer life of Jesus who, according to Luke, would always go off to some place where he could be alone and pray?

Is my prayer dynamism so developed that I too taste and see how good Yahweh is?

Am I so habitually aware of the divine presence within my work and play that I can repeat the psalmist's words, "My eyes are always on Yahweh"?

Has the Lord so taken over my being that I can declare with the ancient Hebrew, "I look to no one else in heaven; I delight in nothing else on earth. My flesh and my heart are pining in love, my heart's love, my own, God forever. My joy lies in being close to God"?

NOTES

1. See, for example, Jn 14:15–17, 21, 23, 26; Rom 5:5; 8:1–28; Eph 1:13–14; 5:19; Phil 2:13; 1 Pet 2:2–5; 1 Jn 4:16.
2. 1 Cor 7:32–35.
3. 2 Cor 3:17.
4. Phil 2:13.
5. Rom 8:14.
6. Decree on the Ministry and Life of Priests, no. 12.
7. Phil 4:4, 7.
8. Lk 8:14.
9. Col 3:1–2.
10. Constitution on the Sacred Liturgy, no. 10.
11. Ps 34:5, 8.
12. Lk 5:16; Mt 6:6.
13. Lk 14:33.
14. Constitution on the Church in the Modern World, no. 31.
15. 1 Tim 6:7–8.
16. 1 Cor 4:15.
17. St. Thomas, in 2 *Ad Cor.*, c. 1., lect. 2a.
18. Hebr 4:12

A Theology of Prayer

Barton W. De Merchant
Detroit, Michigan

Most catechisms define prayer as the "lifting of our hearts and minds to God." While this states a truth, it is easily open to misinterpretation. Two facts easily overlooked in thinking of prayer in these terms are: 1) prayer is an intensely personal action; 2) the initiation of prayer comes from God, not from man.

Prayer is a personal activity: the man who prays must pray as the person he is. When one prays, he addresses himself as a person to God. This excludes a number of activities that are sometimes thought of as prayer simply because they can be fitted somewhat loosely under this general "lifting of heart and mind to God." Prayer is not quiet musing about spiritual subjects. This may at times come close to prayer but it is not prayer because it is not a radically personal activity. Such pious reverie may be nothing more than day-dreaming and as such is only half-conscious activity. If this is considered as prayer, then it would follow that sleep-walking may also be a form of prayer.

Neither is prayer technically that conscious awareness of God one may have as he studies or works. To say that one's "awareness of God's presence" is itself a prayer may be true in a very broad sense. But what is lacking here for genuine prayer is precisely the failure to address oneself as person to God.

Conscious meditation is very close to prayer because it contemplates God, but it usually lacks the deeply personal directedness of the individual who is meditating. Thus, spiritual reverie, consciousness of God's presence, or strict meditation are all technically speaking not prayer, although they may border closely on it. The fundamental ingredient which is usually lacking in any of these is the conscious addressing of oneself as person to God.

Conscious directedness of oneself as person is not an easy activity for most people. To the immature person, in fact, nothing can be more difficult than genuine prayer. The reason for this is somewhat obvious: we only know ourselves by our relationships to others. The person who does not know God by a relationship to him through Christ, cannot know himself. One cannot know himself as son if he does not know God as Father and Christ as Brother. Similarly, without the basic orientation of being related to God through Christ, one cannot see his relationship to others. Without knowing himself as son of God and brother of the Risen Lord, one does not know with any precision what is his relationship to other men.

Because a man does not know his relationship to God and to other men, he does not know himself and therefore does not have the freedom to be himself. Because his relationships are superficial, he is constantly in the act of trying to please others. Often this is nothing more than mere role-playing. And when all of one's activity is a succession of playing various roles, it is impossible for prayer to be really authentic. Rather, it may be the playing of one more role. True prayer can take place only when an individual addresses himself as person to God. This means, of course, that he must know himself so that his prayer can be an expression of himself.

Prayer is also a personal activity in another sense: the God addressed must be addressed as person. Often in prayer the one who prays addresses God as some neutral, non-personal being. Often no particular person of the Trinity is addressed. The prayer is simply to "God" as though one were addressing the divine nature. In speaking of prayer to God, of course, Christians often mean, "God the Father." Or, they mean that they are praying to the Trinity—that is, consciously directing their prayer to the tri-personal Deity. But it is also true that many people address God quite impersonally. They do not think of him as person, but as an abstract, almighty power.

When we speak of addressing God as person, we mean that we address him consciously as Father, Son, or Spirit. We do not merely pray to the Deity. Again, we may address ourselves to the Trinity, that is, we may pray to God as tri-personal, but we must be sure that the word Trinity means "three persons," and not "one abstraction." Because God is one God who is three-personal, no prayer addressed to Father, Son, or Spirit is ever exclusive of the other persons. In fact, all prayer is basically trinitarian and it is the scriptural word and the liturgical action which teach us the way in which we address God as tri-personal. I will treat later on how Christian prayer preserves the distinctiveness of person within the Trinity. My point here has been to lay the foundation that prayer is personal: the man who prays must pray as the person who he is; the God addressed must be addressed as the persons who they are.

Prayer is a dialogue. Everyone agrees with this, but what is often obscured is the fact that it is God who initiates this dialogue and it is man who responds. The popular idea that it is man who initiates this process is a misconception. It is God who wants to impart his own life to men, and for this reason it is he who has spoken first. Our prayer is already answered.

If we stop thinking about prayer in terms of man reaching up to the Deity, then we will solve some of our problems of why God does not answer prayers, that is, why don't we ever hear an answer in return.

On the dust jacket of von Balthasar's *Prayer* we are told that we must stop thinking of prayer as though it were a suppliant's obeisant address to an Oriental despot or the semi-magical incantation of set prayers learned by rote and recited without reflection.

As long as one persists in the fundamental error of thinking that it is man who approaches God, he will persist in an attitude towards prayer which Balthasar describes as ". . . an exterior act performed out of a sense of duty, an act in which we tell God various things he already knows, a kind of daily attendance in the presence of the Sovereign who awaits, morning and evening, the submission of his subjects."

Without revelation, of course, such conclusions would be unavoidable. But that is precisely the point. Revelation teaches us that we approach God as he has already approached us. The very reason why God has revealed himself is so that we may respond to him and know how to come to him.

We have not been left with an uncertainty about who God is or how we are to approach him. It is God who has revealed himself to us and invited our response to his message. The way in which he has revealed himself is, first of all, as Father. And the most complete revelation of that Fatherhood is in the person of Jesus who is the Father's total word. And Christ tells us that it is the Holy Spirit who is given to us as our Spirit who permits us to cry out, "Abba, Father."

Prayer is, therefore, no haphazard affair. It is our response to the revelation that we have received. We respond to the revelation precisely to the Father, through the Son, and in the Holy Spirit.

After Pentecost when the apostles went out to preach the gospel, it is evident that they believed in Christ's divinity (although they would not have had that word). The very fact that they described him as *Kyrios* shows that they considered him equal as God to Jahweh himself. As conscious as they were of Christ's divinity, however, they are even more aware of the fact that it is the Father who has been revealed in the Son. And so, in matters of prayer it is usually the Father who is addressed through the Son in whom they have received their identification as sons and priests. The Father has spoken through the Son. The response is made through the Son to the Father. And this response is possible only because they are "in the Spirit."

From the very beginning, the liturgy reflects this faith. It is directed to the Trinity in this way: to the Father through the Son and in the Spirit. The doxology itself was "*Gloria Patri per Filium in Spiritu Sancto.*" The liturgy was seen as a thanksgiving to the Father for what he had accomplished for his people through his Word and Spirit. The people prayed to God as he had communicated himself to them. The Father had revealed himself fully through the Son. And in receiving the Spirit, they were fully conscious of who they were and of their precise relationship to Father and to Son.

In this connection it is very fitting that in the liturgy the scriptures are read first as the proclamation of God's salvific action, and then only do we respond in thanksgiving. Today, most prayers in the liturgy are still directed to the Father "through Christ our Lord" as our response to the revelation which the Father has made to us through his Son, Jesus Christ. But we can note two shifts present in the liturgy today. The first is the prayer conclusion which specifically mentions the Holy Spirit.

The first Christians were not unaware of the divinity of the Holy Spirit, although it was certainly not precisely formulated in comparison with a Christian's faith-consciousness of today. But they were also aware that the Holy Spirit was their spirit. It was the Spirit expressing himself in their charity and in their worship. In their consciousness of being possessed by the Spirit, they prayed "to the Father through the Son." Eventually the Spirit came to be mentioned more and more by name so that the prayer ending usually included some reference such as "in the unity of the Holy Spirit."

The other and more radical shift which we can observe in the present liturgy is a change in the very structure of the prayers. Today we not only have prayer "to the Father through the Son and in the Spirit," but we also have prayer "to the Father and to the Son and to the Holy Spirit," as well as prayer directly addressed to the Son or to the Spirit.

This shift reflects the Christological and the Trinitarian heresies of the early centuries, especially in reaction to Arianism. Since the expression, "through Christ our Lord," is capable of subordinationist interpretations it was extended to read, "through our Lord Jesus Christ who is living and reigning as God," and then the completion of the Trinitarian formula by concluding "in the unity of the Holy Spirit." What was at one time a simple prayer conclusion, has become a quite detailed creedal formula.

The central point to all this is that no matter whether we address the Father, the Son, or the Spirit or whether we address all three persons together, our prayer is always trinitarian and it is always a response to the way in which God has revealed himself to us. It is the Spirit who has been given us who enables us to respond to the Father through Jesus Christ. And it is in the celebration of the sacraments, especially the Eucharist that we learn to pray.

The old axiom that "the law of prayer" is the "law of faith" (*lex orandi est lex credendi*) is nowhere more applicable than here. True prayer teaches us who the three divine persons are, what they have done for us, and how we can respond to them as the persons they are. The liturgy, of course, is the situation *par excellence* in which we see the Church at prayer.

I would like to apply some of the things we have been saying here to the following specific types of prayer: the divine office, the prayer of intercession, and the prayer of the contemplative.

In regard to the divine office: if Christian prayer is essentially response to God's word, then the Office should be constructed to better exemplify this. As a matter of fact the Office is so constituted in its essentials, but the accretions of the centuries have confused the lines of its basic structure. If we examine the elements of the Office, I think we can find there the model form of prayer outside the sacramental liturgy itself.

Taking Lauds and Vespers as the model hours of the Office, we find the following parts: invocation, psalmody, little chapter, hymn, *Benedictus* or *Magnificat*, gospel canticle (short litany), Our Father, collect, dismissal. What has happened, however, is that the "little chapter" has become too little, and the antiphon at the *Benedictus* and *Magnificat* has become totally truncated. On the other hand, the psalmody has been extended out of all proportion. The psalms were used in worship throughout Christian history, but not in such "big chunks." This idea arose in the monasteries where it was decided to pray all 150 psalms every day in some places. Later, this was spread out systematically over a week. Most short breviaries try to stretch the psalms over the period of a month, or some similar plan. There is a question here of numbers. We can ask the converse question: why stretch them out over anything? We know that some of the psalms would better be used as scripture readings than prayers.

According to many scholars, the office at one time really began with what we call the little chapter, which was a full-length Scripture reading. Following the reading comes the hymn, a response. Then there was a reading of the Gospel followed by a Gospel canticle, another response. Having heard God's word, the assembly prayed. The "Lord have mercy, Christ have mercy, Lord have mercy" litany is really a Prayer of the Faithful concluded by the Our Father and a spontaneous prayer of the leader, later streamlined into a set formula of a collect. Then the dismissal.

Where do the psalms fit into this? According to Jungmann, the psalms were used in two functions: one as a preparation for the readings and prayer, a tuning in. The second reason was that they, along with hymns and canticles, were used in response to readings. This latter is evidenced in the somewhat awkward responses to readings in Matins and Compline.

When the Lauds and Vespers are revised what we will probably have is: Introductory psalm or hymn, Scripture reading followed by hymn or psalm response, perhaps two such readings and psalms and/ or hymns, one from the Old Testament and one from the New Testament, then a Gospel proclamation followed by a canticle. In public celebrations there will be a homily. The idea of a homily is still retained at Matins, but we now read other people's homilies. And we do not read the gospel at all; we say, "At that time, Jesus got into

a boat," and so on, presuming that every one knows the whole peri-
cope by heart.

After the gospel and homily we will have a Litany of Petitions;
having heard God's word, we are sure He can save. He has told us so
in his word. And so, with confidence we go before his throne. After
the Prayer of the Faithful, our leader will summarize our prayers;
together we will say the Our Father; and receive a blessing with perhaps a final hymn.

In other words, the so-called "Bible Vigil" is a return to a more
authentic expression of non-sacramental liturgical prayer than is the
present format of the Office.

In Compline, of course, we have a good outline for community
penance. Reading, confession of sin (general confession), community
act of sorrow and absolution before the formal night prayer begins.
Perhaps this too will once again be brought to life.

How little we have appreciated the Office is shown in the fact that
the laity have been nearly totally estranged from it and have had
exercises of piety substituted. But the religious and clergy did not
appreciate the Office any better, because they have substituted morning and evening prayer, particular examen, spiritual reading, etc. All
these are really provided for in the Office itself if it is unfrozen a bit.

I would like to take now the topic of intercessory prayer under
three aspects: our prayers for others, the prayer of the contemplative,
and our request for the intercession of the saints.

There are certain questions asked today about the purpose of praying for others. Isn't it better to *do* for others? It seems inadequate to
say that God begins to act when we request it. How do our prayers
really affect another?

There are many reasons which can be given for the value of our
interceding for the needs of others. Among them there are:

1) Christ's example and command. This single point is, of course,
   paramount; the command and example of the Lord cannot be
   set aside because of difficulties seen from our limited perspective;
2) We often get bogged down in this when we consider the problem of primary and secondary causality. We are ready to admit
   that God is the final cause, but we also want to pay close
   attention to the more immediate cause, but we also want to
   understand how prayer fits into the ordinary chain of secondary

causes. Once again, though, it seems naive to question a practice only because we do not fully understand how to give a philosophical rationale. Perhaps our whole approach to the question of causality needs expansion, especially our understanding of ourselves as instrumental causes;

3) One very obvious effect of intercessory prayer is the transformation of the one who prays. It makes him more sensitive to the needs of others; it causes him to realize his own creaturehood and God's fatherhood. The prayer of petition makes a man aware of his own dependence;

4) The prayer of intercession also can add great support and consolation to the one prayed for. In this connection, it seems advisable to tell the other person of our prayer and concern. There are some situations which are difficult for us to solve directly. As we hear so much today about showing love and concern for neighbor, we should not belittle the very concrete manifestation of love exhibited in the willingness to take time and effort to remember another in prayer;

5) Hopefully, our prayer of intercession also leads to action. As we contemplate the loneliness of the sick we pray for them. But, if possible, we also visit them. Throughout the Mass we frequently hear some prayer of petition for peace. Perhaps St. Francis of Assisi has expressed this prayer in the most precise theological terms. While most prayers ask: Lord, give us peace, St. Francis says, "Lord, make me an instrument of your peace."

The prayer of the contemplative is a questioned value by some today. And yet, it seems to me to be unmistakably clear that the contemplative is a great sign of faith to men today as in any day. It is also a great sign of concern and love. To give one's life to prayer and penance is a very concrete manifestation of one's commitment to the Lord and to his people.

The Church is a community of persons who should reflect upon the revelation of God, and then order their lives as a response to that revelation. For that reason it makes sense that some persons in the total Christian community are dedicated in a particular fashion to that meditation. There do need to be, however, more direct ways in which the contemplative is able to share the fruit of his meditation with the whole church, so that we may all benefit as the family of God.

Finally, in this area of intercessory prayer I would like to consider in some detail the intercession of the saints in glory. The fundamental error in the minds of many who misunderstand this is that they start at the wrong end. Rather, because they start at the wrong end in regard to prayer in general, they have the whole thing backwards from the beginning. Because prayer seems to be from man's initiative, the whole problem begins with an idea of "my unworthiness in reaching up to God." The saints, in particular the Blessed Virgin Mary, seem to be ways for one to get an "in" with God. Although we are not holy, the saints are confirmed in holiness; the Blessed Mother is the holiest of all creatures. If we can but win the saints to our side, surely they can put in a word for us to God himself.

Such a line of reasoning is, of course, filled with more than one kind of heresy. Since the concern here is with prayer, especially prayer as Trinitarian, I will merely point out the errors in this statement which pertain directly to our problem.

As stated in the first part of this talk, prayer is not man's reach to God, but rather man's response to God's revelation of himself. There is no reason why a man should seek to find ways to go to God, either through the saints or through any other media. The fact is that God has reached out to man. The good news is that Jesus is the revelation of the Father; He, indeed, is the God-man, true God and yet one of mankind.

It is, therefore, not man's problem to find a way to approach God. God has approached man through the Incarnate Son, and revelation tells us that there is no other way to the Father: "For there is one God, and there is one mediator between God and men, the man Christ Jesus." (I Tim 2:5)

An awareness of these truths led the Protestant Reformers to reject all intercession of saints as idolatrous worship, and we must admit quite openly that if the saints are thought of as obstructions between the individual and Christ, or of an approach to God through "some higher channel," or through some person more understanding than Christ (or God himself), then the reformers' accusations are not without a point.

The historical situation of the time gives evidence that the personal responsibility of the Christian had become less and less accented as the expansion of Christendom took place. It became sufficient to be an obedient subject of the ecclesiastical system. The reaction of the

Protestants to this mentality resulted in a complete shift of emphasis. It was not membership in the Church which was important. It was one's personal relationship to Christ as Savior that was stressed; the individuality of the person redeemed was the key soteriological reality. In this context, it was not only the intercession of the saints which seemed to obscure the centrality of the individual's relationship to Christ. The whole sacramental system, including a distinct ministerial (hierarchical) priesthood was called into question for precisely the same reason.

In arguments which did not always bring the core of the problem to the fore, one of the essential ideas really being examined here was the individual vs the community. The Catholic emphasis had been on the communal nature of Christianity. And although we have to admit that there were practices in the Church which indicate that the notion of community at that time left much to be desired, there was at least some awareness that the Christian encounter is basically a community experience. (It is, of course, an individual experience in a sense; but for a truly authentic Christian experience, it is the individual-in-community which is the normative experience.)

Luther's and Calvin's positions were complete reversals: as long as one is individually related to Christ, membership in the Church is optional. This led the reformers to conclude ultimately that the true Church of Christ is "invisible." With their inadequate understanding of the nature of Christian community they were unable to understand any teaching of the Church flowing from that fundamental notion of the Church's nature. Included in this, of course, was a complete inability to accept the intercession of the saints. It is also unfortunate that until recently Catholics have not given really adequate answers to the Protestant objections. In fact, Catholics have often maximized the problem by exhibiting a strenuous "devotion" to the saints without an adequate understanding of what it means to be a Christian.

The fact is that in Baptism the Christian has become a son of God by his identification with Christ as his brother. Through this identification he becomes not a brother in isolation, but one of the Lord's brethren who together are a priestly people. Through confirmation a Christian has become aware that his parish is not the end of the world. Not only is he baptized as a member of a parish community, but Confirmation makes him more aware of the dimension of the whole Church Catholic and how his identity as priest and son of the Father must be active in the realization of the redemption in himself, in the whole household of faith, and in the community of all men. Every time the Christian celebrates the Eucharist, he says "yes" to the commitments of his Baptism and Confirmation.

These realities are fundamental to an understanding of intercessory prayer. One must understand the life of the Trinity, the life of the Christian community and its relation to the Trinity, the Trinitarian prayer of the Christian people, and this, of course, includes the sacraments par excellence.

The saints in glory are enjoying the fulfillment of their Christian lives here upon earth. The vision which they enjoy is not only a Trinitarian experience, but a Christological one first of all. In other words, in eternity the saints know God only "through Christ our Lord." The Christian is not related to the Father indifferently from the way in which he was related to him on earth. He is related to the Father as a "son in the Son." His experience of the Father is possible through his identification with Christ and with the spirit-filled community which is the whole Christ.

The members of the pilgrim church are members of the whole Christ, as are the saints in risen life. This is exactly where intercessory prayer makes sense. The saints in glory are more deeply aware of who they are and who Christ is, and through Christ they contemplate the mystery of the Trinity in its fullness. In this contemplation, they are most deeply concerned for us.

Invocation of the saints is not the seeking of an intermediary with God. The saints are most fully "on our side" of things. They are totally human and they are only human, although it is true that they are humans who have fully realized their ultimate destiny. We approach the saints precisely as members of the same community we are, and we ask that we may experience their prayerful concern for us.

How do the saints hear our prayers? The tradition of the Church indicates that the saints have been invoked (at least in private prayer) since very early times, but there is no clear presentation as to how this is possible. The only real answer we have to this question is the practice of the liturgy. And it is interesting that the liturgy never addresses a prayer directly to a saint. Intercessory prayer follows the same format as the traditional collect: the spirit-filled community prays to the Father through the Son. For example, in this collect the Church prays to experience the intercession of St. Paul:

O God, you see that our trust is not in our own strength: grant then that we may find in the teacher of the Gentiles protection from all evil. Through our Lord Jesus Christ, your Son, who lives and reigns with you in the unity of the same Holy Spirit, one God, for ever and ever. Amen.

This oration is an example of a good formulation of intercessory prayer. The Christian community prays to the Father through Christ. It is deeply aware that physical death, far from destroying the bond between God's people, actually intensifies it. In this prayer, the Church is confident of St. Paul's concern for the rest of us because it is in glorified life that he has overcome all the barriers that heretofore have prevented him from communicating his total love to all of us.

Intercessory prayer of this type is much different from the popular type of devotion which says, in effect: I, as an unworthy individual, try to acquire an ally in the higher echelons to get me a hearing before an aloof deity. Genuine intercessory prayer, on the contrary, says: "I, as a member of a priestly people, have profound identification with the High Priest who is the Second Person of the Trinity. Because he is present to me, the saints are present to me also, for Scripture says, 'they follow the Lamb wherever he goes.'" (Apoc. 14:4) This is, of course, metaphorical in its expression; but it states a valid truth: where the glorified Christ is present, in some mysterious way his glorified members are present too.

In the discussion of intercessory prayer, special consideration must be given to Marian prayer because the Church has traditionally accorded a unique veneration to the Blessed Virgin and this has included the Church's petition for her prayer of intercession.

Veneration of Mary has been a stumbling block in the ecumenical dialogue because for the most part Protestants do not understand the Catholic position in this regard. And it is made worse by the fact that Catholics do not always display a very sophisticated knowledge in this matter either.

To the Protestant, the Catholic devotion to Mary seems to place her as another channel to God, an access to him outside the mediation of Christ. The term *mediatrix* as applied by Catholics to the Virgin has helped to increase confusion in this matter.

The Catholic understanding of *mediatrix* is usually taken in such a way that for all practical purposes, it would seem that Jesus has retired. Having merited the redemption, there seems to be a popular idea that the statement "sits at the right hand of the Father," indicates a completely passive existence on the part of the Redeemer. *Mediatrix* is thought to mean that Christ has turned the distribution of graces over to the Blessed Virgin. This whole subject, of course, is intimately tied up with the opinion that Mary is the co-redemptrix.

The term *co-redemptrix* points to the fact that Mary is a cooperator in her own redemption. Because every Christian is a cooperator in his redemption, he, too, can be called a co-redeemer. In other words, no person is redeemed without his own personal activity involved in the acceptance of the redemption which in itself is completely gratuitous. Mary as co-redemptrix is uniquely co-redeemer, however, because her *fiat* is, in time, prior to the pentecostal church. In this light, then, we can say that at one time the whole church was already founded in Mary, as it were, in microcosm. As the first Christian "before the Church," she is the archetype of the Church, and no subsequent Christian is redeemed in isolation from her.

This notion of co-redemptrix is in marked contrast to the older tendencies (not by any means abandoned in some places) to say that Mary's sufferings actually contributed to the objective redemption, although "in and under Christ."

The term *mediatrix* is seen today to simply stress the idea that all Christians are part of one community, and of the Christian community, Mary is the first Christian in an absolutely unique sense. But the point is, she is absolutely on "this side" of things: that is, she is totally human (in the sense of human only).

The popular expression, "To Jesus through Mary," if correctly understood can tell us that none of us is redeemed in isolation from the community. We will never know the Father except through priestly identification with the Son. And we will not have that identification with the Son except in relation to the whole of the brethren. And, as we have pointed out, among the brethren of Christ, Mary is first and unique.

In conclusion, an understanding of Marian prayer can illustrate everything presented here on prayer as Trinitarian:

1. In her earthly life:
   a) Mary responded personally to God. Mary's life was one of trust and faith, of humble service and total love. In every area of her life she responded to God (and to Christ) as the person she was;
   b) Mary responded to God-as-person. In the *Magnificat*, Mary responds to "God my Savior." She describes herself as the "handmaid." She is open to the Spirit's activity in her. She is the Mother of God's Word Incarnate. She is profoundly identified with Christ's disciples;
2. In her glorified life: Mary prays as the person she is; she prays to God as tri-personal. Her prayer is not between us and Christ; it springs rather from her deep awareness of her total identification with the spirit-filled community. She is the exemplar of what it means to be a cooperator in one's own redemption and a co-operator in making actual the redemption of the world by the revelation of the Father in the hearts of men through the gospel of Jesus Christ.

Our prayer life has suffered because of other difficulties in our theological inadequacies. Let us hope that the renewal of Scripture studies will permit us to know more deeply God's message so that our prayer of response can be more authentic. Let us hope that the renewed studies in Soteriology and Christology will enable us to know better the person of the Risen Lord who leads us to his Father.

Our contemporary stress on the meaning of community should help us to know better who we are as individuals and who we are as the redeemed community of God. This awareness should be reflected in a deeper life of prayer.

Perhaps it is one of the great misfortunes of the history of the Church that prayer came to be classified with fasting, almsgiving, and other mortifications as "penance." This led to the very contradictory notion that on feast days we can be excused from some prayers (*preces*!) and the others we could do "in private" rather than have the added burden (!) of *singing* the Lord's praises. These attitudes are fortunately on their way out as we realize more and more that prayer is our grateful response of praise to the Father's love, manifested to us most of all in his beloved Son.

Let us hope that our fascination with "prayers" as a numerical preoccupation will give way completely to concern with genuine, authentic prayer. And let us determine that the greatest fruit of renewal in religious life will be in the increasing discovery of the richness of a profound prayer-life. Let the religious orders of our day be signs of commitment and prayer to the whole Church: pointing to the larger Church the direction in which it should move if it is to respond to the gospel of Jesus Christ.

The Eucharist as the Foundation of Fidelity in Community

Barton W. De Merchant
Detroit, Michigan

The subject of community obviously cuts across all the social and behavioral subjects. Our limitation here will necessarily be confined to certain theological aspects of community.

Jesus' whole life can be described as a calling of men to community. The very word *ecclesia* means to be "called out." The Scripture affirms that the Christian is one who is called out of darkness into the light. It is also a calling from: from evil and sin, from the "old man." It is a calling for: for the Father, for one another, and for all men. And it is also a calling *together*. Jesus' whole ministry is calling men to live together in peace and brotherhood as they worship the Father and serve their neighbor.

This calling of men is the same process as that which we have traditionally described as Christ's instituting the Church. And Jesus calls men for a certain purpose which can be summarized as a vocation to continue to do what Jesus himself has done throughout his ministry. These specific actions eventually have become known as sacraments. At the very core of all the Church's actions is this continuing to proclaim to men of each generation the invitation to share in the community of Christ—a community empowered in Christ to overcome these obstacles which hinder the possibility of true community being realized.

The Biblical word for community is *koinonia* and means "fellowship," or "communion." It is fundamentally an adjective which describes a certain kind of relationship rather than an organized grouping.

Koinonia is used, first, to express that Christians have a share in Christ and in his benefits. It is first a vertical relationship. God offers man a personal relationship with the Three Divine Persons. This is his offer—flowing from his gracious, merciful love. Our participation is one of response, although a dynamic response. It is a response so deep that we can enter into the action of our own sanctification under the enabling power of the Holy Spirit. *Koinonia* is, then, a realization of a person's relationship to the Father through Christ and his benefits which are communicated to him through the Spirit. It is a sharing, with, in, and through Christ.

But *koinonia* takes on another meaning. It signifies not only the vertical relationship of what an individual person shares in Christ (and in his Father and Spirit), but it secondarily indicates what those who share Christ in common consequently share together. Thus *koinonia* also describes the horizontal relationship. The fellowship I have with Jesus; the communion of life you have with Jesus; this gives us a common bond: namely our life in Him. This common relationship is the foundation of community.

Baptism is the place of initial response to the acceptance of community. It is fundamentally an acceptance of that basic community of life: the Blessed Trinity. In this situation I learn most deeply who I am: son of the Father; brother of Christ; temple of the Holy Spirit. It is here that I am first called to a new people—a people called to combat the "sin of the world" by overcoming sickness and evil and suffering and ultimately death.

We can see very clearly that in Christ's baptism he undertakes to live in total conformity to that identity he has accepted in that public proclamation. Our whole Christian life can be summarized as an obedience to our baptismal vows. Similarly, temptation is the converse. As in Christ's life we see his temptation after baptism consisting in the opportunity to renounce the commitment he had made, we also see temptation in the life of a Christian as the choice to abandon his baptismal commitment.

Baptism is a plunging into Christ's passion and death so that we may live a risen life with Christ. Confirmation should be an expression of an adult person who in full maturity renews the commitment of his baptism: a willingness to worship and serve. It is an adult expression of fidelity to baptism.

The sacrament of penance is a way in which we continue to express the conversation begun in baptism. We are aware today that a Christian is not called to penances, but to penance—to *metanoia*, death to sin and resurrection to new life. We must not settle for token penances, but for total penance: total conversion. As a person realizes those areas of his life which are yet unredeemed, he says in the sacrament of forgiveness that he will continue to be faithful to the process of conversion begun in baptism.

Religious communities should in a very striking manner speak the meaning of Baptism, Confirmation, Penance. The vows of poverty, chastity, obedience, and the living of an intense community life within the total Christian community should point out to all men the meaning of the vocation to which they are called. Chastity should witness to what it means when Paul says "we are constantly being handed over to death for Jesus' sake, that the life of Jesus may be made manifest in our mortal flesh." Consecrated celibacy should really tell us what death to self means. Poverty should remind all Christians of what it means to be a "pilgrim people," to travel light, to be on the move, to be available to go where the action is. Obedience should speak in a very clear way what it means to hear the Gospel and to respond to it with all one's heart. Religious profession should underscore the basic meaning of Christian vocation as evidenced in the sacramental life of the Church. But more importantly, religious profession should be a sign of what it means to be faithful to these realities.

Later, I would like to take up the pivotal point of the Eucharist as the key expression of continued fidelity in community. But before going on to that point I would like to insert a brief consideration of one of the most talked about problems of community today, and one which, in fact, St. Paul himself faced. This is the problem of the tension between the person of talent and the person who holds office; the conflict which may result between the charismatic and the institution.

In 1 Corinthians Paul is aware that community is primarily a sharing. In chapter 12 he speaks especially of the good gifts which the brethren should share. He insists that all gifts (charisms) should be shared in one spirit so that they are always in service to the whole community. He also speaks of those who hold office—the authority which they have and the function which they perform. This, too, must never be used in personal power or prestige but must be a real *diakonia*, a genuine service.

The tension between gift and office is resolved, then, by the fact that both must always be used in one spirit for the good of the whole community. And, Paul then goes on to exhort the brethren to seek after and pray for the higher gifts. In the exercise of those gifts, however, Paul cannot see how any community of gifted and less gifted persons can exist without some kind of structure and officers. He finally says at the end of that chapter: "I will show you a still more perfect way." And then begins the famous hymn to charity in chapter 13. A community of love is his solution to the charismatic-institutional tension.

I have been discussing the meaning of community, some of its problems, and particularly how the sacraments (and religious profession) summon us to be faithful to the Lord in the community to which we have been called. Most of what has been said applies to the whole faith-community, although we have tried to indicate the special significance for the smaller community of the religious institute.

In the final part of this paper I would like to show how the Eucharist sums up the meaning of community and the meaning of fidelity. In relating this to the particular situation of the religious I would like to do it in terms of contrast to the significance of these same values for the married person. (For many of the ideas expressed here, I would like to acknowledge my indebtedness to Brother Joseph Gormley, FSC.)

We have become accustomed to hearing about the consecrated virgin witnessing to the end of time, the *parousia*. The virgin witnesses to the passing away of materiality—even the "stuff" which speaks the meaning of sacraments—to the point when life will be totally Spirit-dominated. And the married person testifies to the fact that the Lord has come in history, he has assumed human flesh, he has lifted all matter to himself, and continues to act today through the instruments of his body, the Church.

This contrast cannot, of course, be pushed too far. The virgin must be caught up in the cares, anxieties and problems of the real world of this moment. And the married person must be an Easter Christian who truly longs for risen life. But on another level, our respective lives have a sign value beyond this instant of time. And it is that deeper meaning which is receiving current attention.

The Eucharist is, of course, the key situation in which we express the meaning of Christ's incarnation and the entire meaning of his birth, death and resurrection. It is also the place where we celebrate our longing for the End-Time and our determination to shape that future in which Christ will be "all in all." In the action of Eucharist each Christian learns what it means to celebrate the Lord's death and resurrection until He comes again and to be faithful to the significance of that celebration.

I would like to treat now complementary aspects of marriage and virginity indicating how each is related to the Eucharist and how each signifies for us the meaning of fidelity in community. I will try to do this briefly from six perspectives.

Covenant. The marriage bond is in itself a revelation of God's covenant with man. In the Eucharist the married couple most fully express the covenant they share with one another and with the Lord. And, in the Eucharistic celebration they also find out what it means to enter into the covenant with the Lord. The virgin, too, is covenanted with God and comes to know most fully what it means to belong to the Lord in the action of the Eucharist. However, the covenant relationship which the celibate experiences is at once more direct and in greater faith-dimension because it is not mediated through the direct love of another person in the same way as in marriage.

Body. Married people come to know what total selflessness means in terms of the giving and the receiving of one another. In the Eucharist they offer themselves as a couple to the Risen Lord, and their relationship to Him is very deep, but always in terms of one another. They receive the body of the Lord and they offer their bodies to Him; their marriage experience has schooled them in what this means. The religious, too, receives the body of the Lord and offers her body to Him, but in a direct fashion which stands in a greater faith-demand on her part. Perhaps an indication of a religious vocation is partly to be evaluated in terms of faith capacity. That is to say, is the religious able to believe that the Lord really loves her without realizing it in as concrete a fashion as does her married sister who has the assurance of God's love symbolized to her through the affection of her husband? This obviously does not mean that the virgin can exist without deep and warm human friendships. It does not mean detachment from others in the sense of aloof exclusion. Detachment in the Gospel means detachment—indeed death—to *self*. The Church community today desperately needs authentic signs of what it means to be crucified totally with the Lord. In the Eucharist the virgin pledges her first affection to the Lord and promises to remain faithful to that vow precisely so that she can more freely serve the body of Christ—the whole community.

Union. Sexual intercourse is an attempt at perfect union with another. I say "attempt," because our sexual urgings can never be completely satisfied and our deepest love can never be adequately expressed. The reason is that we have a longing for "the other" which is infinite. The virgin is a sign that man's completion is in God himself and in Him alone and that perfect union will never take place until we are united to the Lord and to one another in glory. And, the Eucharist is, as St. Thomas Aquinas says, the "pledge of glory." It is the situation where we learn fidelity to our commitment until its consummation in glorified life.

Fruitfulness. In marriage the Christian experiences a peace which drives out fear—a fear which comes from isolation, from lack of proper self-identity, from lack of proper relatedness to others. In marriage I receive the revelation (announced in the Eucharist) that I am deeply loved; I experience the communication of my love to my spouse and to my children. The fruitfulness of the virgin is similar; she has given up physical motherhood in order to be mother and sister to all who need and claim her. In both lives love is absolutely necessary though it may find different expressions. Virginity and marriage do not witness to sex or lack of it—but to love—to the giving and receiving involved in love and proclaimed in the Eucharist "until He comes again."

Community. The Eucharist proclaims community. That is, it says what it is which men are to share: their knowledge; their love; their faith-vision; their common hope of glory. It corrects our notion that Christian couples should share primarily hobbies, recreations, or children. It corrects our notions that the religious should primarily share a common rule, or habit, or horarium. It speaks clearly that what we share is the person of the Lord who gives us his Spirit to form us together so that we may be a unified people who act as a light to the nations in bringing into actuality the redemptive intention of the Father.

The Eucharist proclaims community by saying who the Father is; who Jesus is; who the Spirit is. It calls forth our response to this proclamation. As we respond—we grow in our fellowship, in our sharing. Our community takes expression in our lives as God's people.

But in an even deeper sense our community is rooted in our relatedness to the Three Divine Persons and through them arrives at consciousness of what we share with others.

The Eucharist also proclaims Christ's view of reality: His view of our neighbor; His view of who our neighbor is; His view of who we are. It invites us to accept within ourselves this sharing of Christ's vision.

The Eucharist also expresses community. In our Eucharistic celebration we express our consciousness of the relationships which we bear to the Three Divine Persons and to one another. The Eucharist proclaims that *koinonia* is a sharing in knowledge, love, hope, vision, ultimate destiny. Our act of offering the Eucharist also speaks to what degree we have assimilated that relationship. Our singing, our praying, our preaching, our concern for one another, our feasting at the table of sacrifice speaks exactly to what extent we share the holy things of God by exhibiting to what extent we share with one another the common destiny, the common vision, the common life and love of God our Savior.

And the Eucharist founds community. What we express is always inadequate; what is proclaimed is ever deeper than what is achieved. But if we really listen to the Gospel-word the proclamation falls on more sensitive ears. The proclamation and the expression of our understanding become more closely united so that the relationship which we bear to God and to one another is forming us into a people more and more identified with the revelation which we have received into the meaning of human destiny.

Faithfulness. The Eucharist tells us that God is a faithful God. And that is precisely why we assemble to thank Him. It is in the Eucharistic action that He is with us most clearly. Here He continues to announce that His body is broken for us; His blood is shed for us; His humanity is risen for us; his Spirit is given as our teacher to make plain the Gospel; His promise is made to come again in majesty.

And here we learn to *respond* by our fidelity to Him until death. We learn to be faithful to what we have pledged in Baptism and Confirmation. We learn to be faithful in spite of our need to face our shortcomings. We can even call the Sacrament of Penance a celebration because it celebrates God's fidelity, forgiveness, and love to a people who need constant conversion. In marriage or religious profession a person has more specifically narrowed the area of fidelity and

its terms. In the Eucharist we hear what it is to which we must remain faithful and receive the vision and grace to live that fidelity.

The Eucharist tells us of the community into which we were in-
serted in baptism and which will be complete in the *parousia*. While
we live and hope and press forward to bring to completion that day
about which the baptismal liturgy speaks to each of us:

Receive this burning light and keep the grace of your baptism without
blame. . . . Then, when the Lord comes to the heavenly wedding feast
you will be able to meet Him with all the saints in the halls of heaven, and
live for ever and ever. Amen.

The Meaning and Function of Commitment

REV. THOMAS MORE NEWBOLD, C.P.
Catholic Theological Union, Chicago, Illinois

For a group like ourselves, the very mention of the word commitment evokes a feeling of its importance and a sense of urgency. All our religious communities today are, to some extent, facing the problem of a decreasing number of applicants to the religious life, and feeling the confusion and sadness that come of seeing some (whether few or many) of those already committed, or apparently committed, leave the religious life. Is this phenomenon an unmitigated tragedy? Is it an inevitable trend? Personally, I am convinced that it does not have to be either. In saying this, I am not denying or belittling the fact that our numbers are diminishing, both because of the fewer number of those who seem ready and willing to come into our communities by committing themselves, and the increasing number of those who drop out of our communities by changing their commitment.

In this sense, I wish to recognize the importance and urgency of our discussions during these days. But I would like to specify that importance and qualify that urgency by asking all of you to approach our common concern with the realism of Christian hope and the resilience of a sense of humor. The importance is *not* that of multiplying or increasing our numbers, but of enabling candidates to become themselves in commitment to God in religious community. The urgency is *not* to recruit personnel, but to confirm persons in their commitment to the call that they have from God to the religious life.

I feel confident that if we approach our task of formation with this in mind, the numbers will take care of themselves. Let's face it (and bless God for it) the "numbers game" is over for religious communities. We didn't win it; and we didn't lose it; it's just that we should never have played it. We have a reliable precedent here. Jesus never played the numbers game. As you recall, when He made His great promise of the Eucharist and explained that unless one eat of His flesh and drink of His blood no one would have life, there were many who found this saying too hard to accept. They turned away from Him and walked with Him no more. And Jesus let them go. He even turned to those who were close to Him, His chosen disciples, and asked them the pointed question, "Will you also go away?" In other words, commitment to faith in His providence became the test of discipleship for all, without exception.

One of the many things we learn from this, is that you can't teach or force commitment, any more than you can teach or force a virtue. You can only help it to happen, by motivating it, by encouraging it, by exemplifying it.

By "it" I mean authentic commitment. And to the young candidates who come to us, this means the real thing in a relevant way.

I have just said that we cannot teach or force commitment; but that does not mean that we cannot learn something about it, and then so structure formation that we can help it to happen. If we scale our expectations in this realistic way, then I think we can profitably spend our time discussing it during these next couple of days.

At this point, then, I should like to begin by saying something about the nature, function and experience of commitment.

Nature and Function of Commitment

Existence is not a thing but a *task*. This very important insight was first articulated by the Danish philosopher, Søren Kierkegaard, and it is a very valuable insight, for commitment is the task of existence, inseparably bound up with the personal existence of each one of us.

Because commitment is inseparably bound up with our personal existence, it is, in a very real sense, unavoidable, inevitable. Commitment actually defines in one way or another our state of existence, and that state cannot be what Nicholas Berdyaev once referred to as a state of innocence. By that he meant that state of existence antecedent to choice. This would be a sort of existential vacuum, one in which life would hold for the individual neither meaning nor value.

It is of the very nature of commitment to choose, to decide the way

I shall exist. Many aspects of my existence are such that I had and have no choice or decision to make, for example, *that* I begin to exist *when* I come into existence, my sex as a male person, etc. But once I have this gift of existence, it is mine to choose and to decide the way I shall exist as the person I am in the world I am in.

The existentialist psychologists are fond of calling existence "A Project." It is, and a very personal one; one whereby, through choice and decision, I give shape and direction to my whole life and living, to my entire existence. This is why commitment is not only by its very nature a matter of choice, but also by its very nature a matter of basic choice, a primordial auction. The first, the most basic choice facing anyone who accepts the task of existence is the supreme choice which will give a consistent orientation to his whole personal existence, and in the light of which all other choices will be made. When we say "first," we obviously mean it not in a temporal sequence but in a psychological and theological sense, since we frequently make many specific decisions before the absolute choice. It is well to remark here the important fact that one cannot revoke a genuinely basic choice with impunity, because such a choice engages our whole destiny, both temporal and eternal. That such a choice involves grave risks is certain, and this is why many hesitate before making it. And yet, as long as a person has not made his absolute choice, his basic choice, and has not committed himself or herself irrevocably, he or she will have no means of concentrating and integrating his scattered life forces and energies on a central axis. And the consequence of this will be that such a person will not be able really to achieve the task of his or her existence in an authentic way.

In speaking of the nature of commitment as a basic choice, it is also necessary to note that some values of existence can only be chosen absolutely. This, of course, is primarily true of religion, used in the highest sense of the word, namely, the bond which unites man to God. It simply is not possible to be half Christian and to be really Christian. As Kierkegaard wrote, "Many strange, deplorable and blameworthy things have been said about Christianity, but the most stupid thing ever said was that it was true up to a certain point." Either Christianity is true or it is false; but it cannot be one or the other, except absolutely. As we know, St. John, in the Apocalypse, said the same thing when he wrote that God requires us to be hot or cold, but if we are tepid, he will spew us out of His mouth. What this powerful, and in some respects terrifying, image of Scripture tells us is simply that the basic choice of our life commitment must be an absolute choice, a primordial option.

Now, I think it should be quite obvious that the choice we make in committing ourselves to religious life is not identical with this absolute choice of God; but it is so closely connected with it that it must share its absolute quality and character. The reason for this is simple enough. The function of religious commitment is to incarnate, to enflesh, my primordial choice; to give it historical visibility in an affirmation of love that is total and permanent. This is why an authentic commitment to religious community is never made lightly, nor terminated casually. For its function is to make of the primordial option an enduring reality.

The task of existence is a human reality; and like everything else that is human, it must be accomplished in the human dimensions of time and decision and effort. Religious commitment needs to recognize human reality. Precisely because we are not automatons, we cannot pretend that one gesture, one act, or one programming is enough. There is no present that can constitute a stopping point, just as there is no past which can be considered as something over and done with. Our present is our constant effort towards the future; it is laden with the past, and transforms it endlessly. Religious commitment, then, is a love affirmation, a saying "Yes" to God, made initially but continually deepened, expanded and expressed.

All of this, it seems to me, is reflected powerfully and pervasively throughout the Scriptures. The Bible is the book of choice and decision. From end to end it sets man face to face with the supreme choice which determines all the other choices in his life; from the law of Moses: "I have set before you life and death, therefore choose life" (Deut. 30:19), to the word of Christ: "No man can serve two masters" (Matthew 6:24). In each and all of the personal confrontations of which the Bible is full, the word of God speaks to man, making him a person, a responsible being who must answer. Commitment is thus the human response to the divine invitation.

Commitment as Human Experience

In thinking about the nature and function of commitment, we have noticed that it is a human reality. It will, therefore, be experienced as such. I would like now to make some observations on the way religious commitment is experienced.

I should like to begin with the quotation from the Constitution on the Church (#46): "Everyone should realize that the profession of the evangelical counsels, though entailing the renunciation of certain values which undoubtedly merit high esteem, does not detract from the genuine development of the human person. Rather by its very nature it is most beneficial to that development."

Undoubtedly, in making this statement, the fathers of Vatican Council II met head-on the objection to religious commitment that, to the contemporary mind, is the most plausible and carries the greatest urgency. It is an objection that is bound up with the psychologically unsound assumption which asserts that a person must somehow experience everything for himself or herself, before he or she can choose or decide anything freely. It takes but a moment of thought, I believe, to realize that this is not only a psychologically unsound assumption, but also a physical impossibility. Yet it is behind the attitude of those who object to any definite commitment, whether it concerns the indissolubility of marriage or the dispensation of religious vows, involving as these do promises of loyalty or fidelity. It is the denial of those who claim that it is metaphysically impossible for a person to commit himself or herself, or to be faithful, with assurance that such commitment is authentic. If, in fact, human existence is only a succession of phenomena and psychological states,—if what I am today has not real relation with the man who will bear my name tomorrow, in a month, or in some years time; if "I" is only a semantic fiction, then obviously no commitment is possible, and any promise of fidelity would be an absurdity. For how could I commit another, or ask another to keep my promises? The only logical conclusion that can be drawn from this is the inevitable bankruptcy of all human existence.

Authentic human existence is possible only if I accept choice, commitment, constancy and fidelity as existential values. It is only thus that there can be the realization of an existence, of *my* existence. The "I" is not a simple semantic fiction; it expresses my personal reality. In spite of all physical and psychological changes which have taken place, I am the same person today as the man who, 25 years ago, committed himself to a certain vocation, swore loyalty and fidelity to a particular religious community.

Many of our contemporaries are afraid of a choice involving a commitment and implying fidelity, because they fear it will involve giving up one of the values which today is very highly esteemed, that is, non-involvement. Always to be able to get away, to be ever responsive to new experiences, never to refuse any possibility, this is the plausible philosophy of complete non-involvement. It is given classical expression by André Gide in his book *Les Nourritures Terrestres*. The character Menalcus, in Gide's novel, is a man who refuses to choose lest he make a miscalculation and amputate something of himself. His attitude toward life is one of passive expectation, one that refuses and is fearful of any renunciation because he might miss some experience.

There is a deadly error at the root of this conception of non-involvement. True non-involvement derives not from the spirit of possession, but from poverty. If we consider the world and our fellowmen as belonging to us, or revolving around us, we can obviously not commit ourselves and still keep our state of non-involvement. Actually, however, I should never try to possess others. Even my own person does not belong to me, and I am not the center of the universe. It is I, rather, who belongs to the rest of the world. I am certainly accessible to the summons of God, but not passively. God, the world, and my fellowmen do not demand that I suffer them passively, that I offer them up, but they expect from me exactly that creative fidelity, that free choice, that commitment and loyalty and constancy which are sometimes so difficult, but always necessary. The real name for the truly and authentically non-involved person, is detachment. That is to say, one who is not encumbered with self, is capable of that subordination of his own interest to the common good and to the whole, of that detachment from what he has and what he is, which are indispensable to an authentic commitment, and to a fidelity which is not mere routine.

In the light of these reflections, I think it is rather easy to see that commitment will have to be experienced sometimes as *renunciation*, and religious commitment as *definitive* renunciation. The very experience of commitment as fidelity and constancy is impossible without some experience of renunciation. To commit oneself is to choose, and choosing always means renouncing. It means defining our very person and shaping our very life by abandoning resolutely whatever cannot be integrated into the central and controlling commitment of our existence.

The reason for this is simple and profound. The task of existence is more necessary than having any given experience, more important than the fulfillment of any given talent. Those people who have the insight that experience is a very important and necessary thing, do not seem to realize this simple fact when they make a cult of experience itself. The very meaning of experience is lost and its reality is prostituted or debased if it means experimenting with existence, rather than commiting oneself to existence.

In every life that is really lived the task of existence is achieved, and the integration of the self is accomplished only when the person concerned is ready to discard certain modes of existence which are not compatible with that commitment that gives basic orientation to his or her life. To give a simple example: A college boy may develop a mode of existence which permits him to date a number of girls enthusiastically. But as soon as he decides to marry one of them, he must give up dating the others. As Chesterton said rather wittily: "One cannot enter the Garden of Paradise through all four gates at once." In other words, to commit oneself to a basic mode of existence always implies some renunciation, some detachment from other modes of existence. All authentic commitment implies renunciation. Just as involvement is pervaded by mortification, and freedom implies discipline, so commitment demands renunciation. All involvement, any form of loyalty, and swearing of fidelity involves us in the renunciation of values, sometimes very important to us, but values which are incompatible with the nature of our primordial option.

There is something sad and depressing in the spectacle of those persons whose lives become a constant state of agonizing hesitancy about making the decision in favor of certain modes of existence with their concomitant exclusion of others. For such persons, the task of existence will become ambiguous, inconsistent, fraught with conflict, weak and whimsical. Ultimately it tears the person to pieces psychologically. He becomes restless; he does not know why he is where he is, why he is doing what he is doing, or where he is going. His life becomes a shapeless, amorphous mass, even if it does not eventually become a disastrous mess.

What such persons do not seem to realize is that it is only by commitment, by actually committing themselves, that one releases the energies of life, opens up its possibilities, finds its personal meaning, and realizes its worthwhile goals.

Thus, there is a very important and paradoxical corollary to the ex-

perience of commitment as renunciation. It is the fact that the renuncia-
tions of commitment lead not to an impoverished but to an enriched
existence. The paradox is simply an instance of that which our Lord
Himself spoke of when He said: "He who loses his life for my sake
shall find it." It is only when a person is unable to give up something
that he loses everything. If he tries to keep open all possibilities of life
he realizes no possibility. Yet the fact remains that when commitment
is strong and dynamic, the incompatible modes of existence lose neither
their meaning nor their appeal. In the beginning they may still have an
overwhelming attraction. Such an experience is normal and should not
lead to guilt or shame or anxiety. What happens is simply that the excluded modes of existence need no longer participate in the daily self-
actualization of one's chosen commitment. They recede more and
more into the background; day by day they lose a little more of their
appeal. But they are not repressed. They are not forcefully ejected
from one's existence; neither is their presence denied. They are simply
taken for what they are: beautiful, valuable, attractive possibilities of
existence which are no longer needed because they are no longer in
harmony with the chosen orientation of one's own task of existence.
It is thus that the truly committed person learns to appreciate deeply
and enjoy immensely the existential values in the lives of others, even
though those values no longer play a role in his own life. One feels no
need to depreciate or belittle them; one need no longer deny their presence or their value. One simply develops the capacity to appreciate
and to enjoy the value of those things which he cannot have or does
not need. And so it is that authentic commitment is compatible with
fullness and wholeness, but not with non-involvement, with a dabbling
dilettante experimentation with existence. Authentic commitment is
compatible with the unforeseen, with doubt, with temptation, with
honest perplexity; but it is not compatible with living provisionally,
perpetually.

Conclusion

By way of conclusion I should like to make just one further point,
because I think it can often lie at the very heart of any commitment, in
the form of a nagging doubt or hesitancy. The point is this: in the experience of commitment, disappointment and infidelity are always pos-

sible in principle, but need never be the lasting, actual condition of existence. Allow me to explain that just briefly.

Because our commitment must always realize itself in time, and because temporal duration itself is not a smooth mechanical development but a daily creation, our task of existence, no matter how we view it, is always vulnerable. On the basis of my limited knowledge of myself and of my future, as well as on the basis of my own finite resources, I always know that I simply cannot predict with perfect assurance that I shall make a commitment total or that my fidelity will be permanent. Taken simply as my human determination to be consistent, or as my willingness to be subject to social restraint, the ground of my commitment is necessarily precarious. But when my commitment is centered on God Himself, invoked as the eternally faithful, then the ground of my fidelity becomes unshakable. For my commitment to be real and authentic, it must be based on a humble appeal delivered from the depths of my own insufficiency to Him Who is the eternally faithful. Gabriel Marcel, I think it was, called this the absolute resort. It is an appeal which presupposes a radical humility in the one who makes a commitment, a humility which is polarized and stabilized by the very transcendence of the One Whom it invokes. It is an appeal which puts my whole existence at the juncture of the most demanding commitment and the most reliable expectation. It cannot be a matter of counting on one's self, on one's own resources to cope with the unbounded commitment of a life choice. But if in the act in which I commit myself, I at the same time extend an infinite credit to God to Whom I commit my life, then I have the assurance of Christian hope. It is on this ground, and on this ground alone, that all fidelity to commitment becomes possible, and that any commitment finds its guaranty. It is for this reason, and for this reason alone that we recognize the meaning and value of commitment as *consecration.*

The assurance of Christian hope can come to us only by the acceptance of existential risk. Humanly speaking, such risk is often folly, but it is the folly of the Cross. It is also the only way for man to emerge from his egoism and from his small and narcissistic universe. It puts an end to the spirit of possession, to the false security of inauthentic routine, and demands that we live in readiness and hope. How wearisome, after all, and how lacking in tragic intensity and passionate splendor would be the life of one who was granted the power to foretell and forestall his future. Knowing ourselves exposed to risk, we put our trust not in ourselves but in God, hoping that he will stretch out his helping hand to free us. It is evidently not in passive waiting or in panic and hesitancy, but in courageous and confident commitment, that we expose ourselves to risk, and thereby gain the assurance of Christian hope.

Ultimately, commitment is man's capacity to receive the gift of unassailable hope from God the Faithful One. The need to be self-sufficient underlies most of the anxiety and hesitancy which makes us hold back or break a commitment. Crucial to our courage in the time of testing is our capacity not only to give, but also to receive the gift of hope from God. The Apostle Paul articulated the real concept of commitment when he said: "We rejoice in our sufferings, knowing that suffering produces endurance, and endurance produces character, and character produces hope, and hope does not disappoint us, because God's love has been poured into our hearts through the Holy Spirit which has been given to us." (Rom. 5:3–5)

Experience of Commitment and the Structure of Formation

Rev. Thomas More Newbold, c.p.
Catholic Theological Union, Chicago, Illinois

In the preceding paper, I had quite a bit to say about the experience of commitment, but it was largely a descriptive analysis. What I should like to do now is to make an attempt to put all this in a more practical context, by discussing commitment in terms of the experience of the candidates who come into a formation program. It is both the factors of experience which they bring *to* formation, and the experience they have *in* formation that condition their experience of making a commitment at all.

Factors of Experience Brought to Formation

The first factor which it will be profitable for us to consider, is simply an all-pervasive fact familiar to us as members of an older generation in our relationship to youth. The young people of today, whether we like it or not or whether we accept it or not, insist that they are doing a new thing. They proclaim themselves children or citizens of a new age, even as they reject the claims made on their lives by those "over thirty." This, I would presume, would mean an attitude toward most of us here present. If the young of today seem to exaggerate their sense of discontinuity with preceding generations, it is because they are conscious of their unique historical situation and anxious lest they simply repeat the failures of their forebears. They sense that it is their task to discover values and to elaborate life-styles appropriate to a rapidly changing culture, dominated by technology and conditioned by crowded living quarters of an urban nature, with an abundance of leisure time. They sense instinctively that the survival of the human species requires radical adaptation to a rapidly changing environment.

This indiscriminate repudiation of the past, characteristic of so many contemporary young people, may well cause as many problems as it solves. These are problems for the young themselves, as well as for those of us in the older generation who have to relate to them. An exclusively negative and critical appraisal of heritage and tradition always tends to frustrate the need for cultural roots and for communal identity. Lacking confidence in traditional solidarities—the home, the college, the church, the religious community, the nation, and even the world in general, the young turn to the peer group as the single locus of significant experience. Thus it is that many young people today suffer the loss of a reflective reference to the past, to the funded experience of our human race and the human condition. Issues displace ideologies, and history is replaced by the "happening" as a matter of compelling interest and concern. When a young person, whether male or female, participates deeply in these general contemporary attitudes of youth, it becomes a live option for them to tune-in or cop-out on existence generally. At least, they are often tempted to do so, and show all the elements of rebelliousness, indifference, and lack of concern that go with such an attitude.

There is another very personal factor of experience the contemporary candidate brings into the formation process of the religious life, and I think it is extremely important that we all try to understand it. This is an attitude of searching indecision and sometimes agonizing uncertainty which we must be careful not to read as indifference and unconcern. It is connected with the crisis of identity about which we hear so much today. I believe it has been best described by the psychologist who has researched it most, Dr. Erik Erikson. Dr. Erikson has given it the now popular and well-known technical name: "Psycho-social Moratorium."

What Dr. Erikson means by this psycho-social moratorium, is this: Cultural anthropologists, in contrasting the youth situations of earlier cultures, notably in primitive societies, with our own, have found a very great difference in the cultural status of young people of today. In earlier times and cultures it was much simpler to pass from youth to adulthood, though that does not mean that it was much easier. It does appear that in earlier cultures there was hardly any discernible youth sub-culture such as we have today. Transition to full membership occurred rather smoothly, in an orderly and traditional way, legitimized by very significant rituals. Initiation brought the young person fully into society; his status was accepted early, and he enjoyed full participation and responsibility. It was thus that the energies of youth were rather smoothly and quickly incorporated into the wider society, which tended to absorb them easily and early, before they could be identified sharply or given a chance to become rebellious or revolutionary. Such societies, for these and other reasons, tended to remain relatively changeless and static.

In modern society, we have a somewhat different picture and condition. Increasingly in contemporary society, with its strongly economic-oriented value system, the young person goes through a prolonged marginal status which tends to suspend his sense of identity. Thus, today, one can hardly hold down a decent job without at least some college degree. Thus also, until well into the 20s the young person of today, both male and female, is kept in a state of dependence, both parental and environmental. Thus, suspended commitment and marginal identity go together as part of the experience of today's young person.

Now this is all very well, except that it confronts the young person with a multiplicity of possible commitments and choices of vocation at that very point in the schedule of his individual growth which finds him eager to realize actual roles which promise him eventual recognition within the many possibilities of vocation and career in our culture. As we all know, the young person of today has access to a broad range of information both before and after he takes the first steps into religious life. This pluralism of possibilities shows him that there is no single way of becoming a full person, or of serving God and God's people. He enjoys multiple contacts with accumulated knowledge and speculation, and from them he learns possible alternatives for his choice of a vocation and/or career.

So many options and opportunities lie before the young person today, that he tends to be, if not indecisive, at least tentative about things. Afraid to tie himself to the wrong value or bet on the wrong horse, he is inclined to "keep his cool," not to go overboard. During his prolonged marginal status of dependency, he has developed habits of critical appraisal which make him inclined to withhold a too easy assent; he has seen too many people commit themselves too quickly, only to turn back.

However, we must be careful not to read this indecision and uncertainty in the young as indifference and unconcern. Actually what is at work here is the specific strength inherent in the age of youth. It is the sense of and the capacity for fidelity amid diversity. In the basis of individual growth, fidelity could not mature earlier in life and must not, in the crisis of youth, fail its time of ascendance, if human adaptation and mature commitment are to happen. It is for this reason that Dr. Erikson remarked: "In no other stage of the life cycle, are the promise of finding one's self and the threat of losing one's self so closely allied."

One can see evidence of the functioning of this capacity for fidelity, this potential for commitment in young lives in their search for something and somebody to be true to, in a variety of pursuits more or less sanctioned by society. This search is often hidden in a bewildering combination of shifting devotion and sudden perversity—sometimes more devotedly perverse, sometimes more perversely devoted. Yet, in all youth's seeming ambivalence, a seeking after some lasting and durable commitment among the diverse possibilities of existence can be detected. One can see it in their desire for accuracy of scientific information or technical matter, or in their desire to experience sincerity of conviction, authenticity of personality, and reliability of commitments. This search is easily misunderstood, and often it is only dimly perceived by the individual himself, because youth, always set to grasp at and test diversity, must often test extremes of existence before settling on a considered course. These extremes, particularly in times of confusion and change like our own, as well as in the widespread experience of the marginality of identity, may include sometimes rebellious, deviant, and even self-defeating tendencies. However, all this can be, and should be in the nature of a moratorium, a period of delay, in which to test the rock-bottom of some possibility of existence before committing the powers of body and mind and heart to a segment of the existing (or a coming) order of things. It is in this context, that Dr. Erikson remarked very well, "Loyal and legal have the same root, linguistically and psychologically; for legal commitment is an unsafe burden unless shouldered with a sense of sovereign choice, and experienced as loyalty."

Thus, we should not be surprised, discouraged or impatient when we find that the young can say clearly what he as yet cannot live. We may think at times that the young person is unduly prolonging the moratorium, and so it may be. It can happen that some young people, when faced with the diversity of possibilities in their existence, may retreat from or put off commitment, by conjuring up systematically the full range of possible alternatives for existence, and then claiming that they must test them one by one before they can make their commitment. However, it does not take long for the young person to realize that this is both a physical and psychological impossibility. Nevertheless, what this impossible attempt implies is that the young person is experiencing the need to develop a sense of identity from among all possible and imaginable relations. He finally realizes that he must make a series of ever narrowing selections of personal, occupational, sexual, and vocational commitments. Here we see that diversity and fidelity are polarized. They make each other significant, and they keep each other alive. Fidelity without a sense of diversity can become an obsession and a bore; diversity without a sense of fidelity, can become an empty relativism.

Now this capacity for fidelity amid diversity, this potential for commitment, is that specific strength of the young which can emerge only in the interplay of the experience of an individual and the social forces and structures of a true community. That capacity for loyalty, for legal commitment, experienced as loyalty, must be developed as the blending of the individual's life history and the inspirational power of a religious community.

Factors of Experience in Formation

With that I should like to turn now to a discussion of the factors of experience which the contemporary candidate will have, should have in formation. I shall confine the discussion to just one factor, namely, the need for the experience of authentic community. Community is perhaps the most widely used term in recent discussions about religious life and religious formation. It evokes in some, feelings of great expectation and excitement, as well as feelings in others of utter boredom. For the moment, therefore, I am going to try to avoid this word in order to take a more critical look at the underlying dynamics of community. I should like to further focus or limit our discussion by making a somewhat critical examination of two new approaches in religious formation which have become very popular in practically all modern seminaries and religious communities in both the United

States and Europe. I will refer to these as dialogue and small-group living, and although it may be found somewhat disconcerting as well as provocative of discussion, I propose to examine these new methods with a view to indicating some of the most overlooked complications they contain. It is important, I think, that I say at this point that I do not try or intend in any way to question or minimize the value of these methods. It remains true that experiencing authentic community in an authentic way brings to resolution the crisis of identity, releases the potential for fidelity, and enables the making of that total and permanent commitment which is proper to the religious life. I wish to point out, however, some of the many hidden facts of which we in formation must be aware in order to avoid them.

First I shall discuss dialogue, using the word in a very general way. It is meant to designate many forms of behavior, described in such terms as: encounter, open discussion, talking things through, being open to each other, and it indicates a high level of oral communication. In my brief discussion here I should like to focus on the oral aspects of the dialogue.

The growing emphasis on the value of oral communication of students and candidates to the religious life with each other and with those in charge of their formation, is based on two presuppositions, both of which presuppositions are usually unarticulated, and both of which are commonly taken for granted. They are, first: that free and open sharing of ideas and feelings brings people closer together; and, second, that a high degree of oral interchange facilitates existential decisions by clarifying the issues involved.

The first question we ask, therefore, is: Does oral communication actually bring people closer together? Although words are meant to communicate, they are very often used as a curtain to prevent communication. In many discussions, words are used to fill a painful and fearful silence, to prevent the real questions from being asked or the painful issues from being touched. Many parliamentary discussions are, as we know, aimed more at delaying the problem than at coping with it. Hours of endless talk in the United Nations Assembly seem to an outsider to be trivial and superficial; yet they fulfill the highly useful function of preventing dangerous and explosive encounters.

This is obvious on a large scale, but we are seldom aware of these same dynamics operating as we encourage candidates to discuss their problems. Let us not forget that candidates, particularly candidates in formation, know that they are constantly subject to evaluation, and as a result are in many ways afraid of each other as well as overly self-conscious. They are often so caught up in questioning their own adequacy that they are reluctant to allow anyone to enter into the sensitive area of their personality, where they themselves experience doubts and confusions. When you sit in and observe carefully a discussion among students or candidates to the religious life, you will often find yourself feeling that the whole situation is restrained and confined within the verbal coil of language. The more words used, the more restraining the discussion becomes.

Now what I am trying to say is that oral interchange between students in a seminary, or candidates in a novitiate does not always bring them closer together; it might separate them. Candidates who have been encouraged to engage in dialogue, with the suggestion that this will create a better community, can become very disappointed and even hostile when they find that months, and perhaps a whole year, has not taken away their feelings of loneliness and alienation. Often enough they find an unexpected and disappointing contrast between the results of many discussions, and the main reason for engaging in them. Sometimes they feel more like strangers after than before the dialogue started. It is not difficult to see how feelings of failure and depression can come from such an experience, and it may well be followed by an emotional conviction which is articulated as: "This life is not for me."

A second question which I think we may legitimately examine here is: How far does the clarification of pertinent issues by way of discussion help to solve existential problems? Here I believe we touch upon something which can be a source of prolonged frustration and painful indecision. The reason is simply that insight into a problem, and the ability to cope with it are two entirely different things. If candidates discuss the meaning of the religious life, celibacy, the institutional church, the death of God, and so on, this might help them to think more clearly about these issues and to see the different ramifications of the problem, but if they expect to solve their very personal questions: Should I become a religious, vow a celibate life, remain within the institutional church, and believe in a living God—then long discussions can become an excruciating experience. I myself have had the experience of following a year-long discussion by seminarians who hoped to make a decision on celibacy before the approaching date

of ordination. It was really sad to see how many of these students became more and more entangled in a complex pattern of arguments,
ideas and concepts; and found themselves lost in a labyrinth of theological turnpikes, highways, and side roads—with mounting frustration and growing anger over the fact that they never came to that
mysterious center where the answer was supposed to lie waiting for
them.

What is it that is really happening here? Instead of entering into a
long dissertation on the subject, I would simply ask you: What would
you think about a boy and girl spending an hour a day to find convincing arguments that they love each other? Probably such discussions
would be the best argument that they should not marry each other,
if they do not want to enter into a rigid, frigid, stiff relationship, with
a total lack of spontaneity.

Very briefly, I may put it this way. Discussion means a certain distance from the subject, which allows you to see the many aspects of
the issues involved and gives you the opportunity to be analytical about
these issues. But discussion and analysis mean a temporary delay of
participation. And only on the level of participation are existential decisions made. Nobody becomes a priest or religious because of three or
four convincing arguments. Nobody commits himself or herself to
the celibate life, for instance, because of a reading and discussion of
Rahner, Schillebeeckx, or Sydney Callahan. Theology, psychology,
and sociology do not offer solutions for existential crises; and anyone
who suggests they may enhances frustration, especially in the case of
the young, who have not yet fully experienced the limitations of sheer
reasoning and the necessities of human existence.

Here I should like to mention, parenthetically, a tragi-comic note
which I offer without any desire or intent to be facetious or cynical.
It is the fact that, while in many seminaries and houses of formation
there is a growing adulation for explicit intellectual awareness and an
increasing emphasis on the sensitivity of "knowing what you do," the
non-religious youth is burning incense, practicing transcendental meditation, and smoking pot, to reach a higher degree of participation with
the basic sources of life. Meanwhile, in many of our seminaries and
formation houses, our liturgies have become more talkative and
verbose, and incense and other sense stimuli, auditory and visual, are
scorned as being part of an old magic and past tradition.

This is rather amusing, perhaps, but it is also serious, in the sense that it highlights the necessity of real participation in existence as it is, in order actually to make an existential decision. We can, and we should, by all means, encourage dialogue. But we must see to it that the candidates for religious life do not feel caught in the endless coils of their own discussions and dialogues and, seeing no end in terms of decision making, become disappointed. Their disappointment may very well lead to their disappearance. They may, in their own language, simply give up and "cop out" on the possibility of a vocation to the religious life.

Along with a growing emphasis on dialogue and discussion, we find in many formation programs today a shift from large, sometimes anonymous, groups of candidates living together in one building, to the more intimate, small groups, often called teams or task forces or core groups.

This approach to formation is an obvious, and I think, healthy reaction to a very impersonal kind of living in which the candidates went through one or several years of formation without ever being able to establish meaningful relationships, either with their fellow candidates or with the formation personnel. By dividing the large group into small teams, the possibility of real human relationships at a deeper level is created and a new form of community living is envisioned. But here too, just as in the case of dialogue and discussion, things do not always work out in the expected direction. Allow me to discuss very briefly some of the difficulties and perhaps hidden traps involved in this small-group approach.

I think the first problem is the simple fact that the candidates, in such a small group approach, cannot avoid each other any longer in a normal and human fashion. In a large group where small, informal sub-groups usually develop quite naturally, there is a possibility of staying away from irritating people, to simply take a distance from others who seem to operate on a different wave length, and to move more or less freely in and out of the large group. In a team or small group, you are very close to others, and many of your activities are under the critical eye of the other group members, even when you do not, at least at times, feel attracted to them. If you do not show up for a meeting, this not only will be noticed, but possibly criticized as indication of lack of interest or commitment to the group. If you do not speak in a group session, people wonder why you are so silent. Whatever you do or do not do can become highly charged with personal connotations. It is obvious, therefore, that small group living is much more demanding than living in a large group, and calls for a much greater maturity. This is good, but it is not always possible at any given time for every individual who decides to join the group.

A second problem is related to the confusion about the meaning of a team or small group. The word team or core group is ordinarily used to indicate the cooperation of a small group of people who coordinate their different skills in order to be better able to fulfill a certain task. The common task is what determines the nature of the team or small group.

In a formation setting, however, the small group often is not task-oriented. The group wants to create the best possible living conditions for its members. It is more like a family unit to which one returns after a busy day of work. Here the problems start, because the small group in this setting easily becomes self-oriented instead of task-oriented; the problems of the group are no longer related to questions raised by the nature of the work to be done, but to questions raised by the nature of the interpersonal relationships. It is in this context that many small group meetings, especially in a formation context, tend to degenerate into amateur group therapy in which members try to explore their feelings towards one another and to encourage each other to put on the table many things which might better remain in the drawer. In cases such as these, small group meetings can become highly charged, and instead of moving away from individual concerns to a common concern and task, they can become self-centered to the point of narcissism.

What I have said so far on this problem may appear to be very critical in a negative sense. For this reason I should like to explain it further. We must realize that the candidates involved in a formation program are already very self-conscious, relative to their age, their academic life, and their ambivalent feelings toward their future commitment. Although it might be very important, even necessary, that individual anxiety, confusion and depression be expressed at certain times, the main purpose of the formation program is to encourage candidates to grow away from this self-interest and to become free and open— to be really interested in the life and concerns of others. Jesus Himself expressed this basic, sound psychological necessity when he said, "You must lose your life in order to find it."

It is quite true that a culture, or a type of religious community life, which does not allow regression at times can ruin personality. Without some sleep a man cannot live, but it is well to remember that the vital things in life usually do not happen during sleep. Crying, talking about oneself, and defenseless expression of feelings of love and hate may be very important for the mental health of an individual, but they are all temporary regressions which can only be meaningful in terms of ensuing progression. The formation regression should be allowed and even encouraged at times, but never considered as an ideal to strive for. The ideal remains: not to be overly concerned with self, not to cry, not to express all emotions indiscriminately, but to deny oneself, to learn to cope with problems alone at least occasionally, and to do work which calls for attention and interest even though the emotions may not always be consonant with that attention and interest. Therefore, I feel very strongly that a formation program using the small group approach, and in which regressive forms of behavior are encouraged as the ideal or even encouraged as the predominant expression of community, is vitiating its own purpose.

A third problem that is always somehow involved with small group living approach in formation, is the common one related to intimacy. As we all know, loneliness is often experienced on a very deep and at a very painful level by young people, and the tendency exists to look for a solution for this problem by establishing very demanding and often exhausting friendships. These friendships can be clinging, immature, and based, oftentimes, on an unconscious expression of primitive and infantile needs. One of the tasks of formation is to stimulate the candidate not to let himself or herself be guided by these impulsive needs, but to come to a mature self-awareness and self-confidence, in which real, warm, and profound friendship can develop as a giving and forgiving relationship, one in which feelings of loneliness can be understood and accepted in a mature way.

Intimacy is not community. And it is therefore very important to guide the group experience in such a fashion that it does not become a clique which is allowed to act on, and to act out very primitive needs and desires in an indiscriminate fashion. This is difficult, because the stresses and tensions of many candidates are so intense that they often have inexhaustible needs for intimacy and for clinging friendships. To encourage this, is often to encourage the unrealistic fantasy that the true, real, faithful friend is somewhere waiting, able to kiss away all feelings of frustration. A person who lives in a religious community or vows himself to religious life with this fantasy is doomed to be a very unhappy person. And if the small-group living approach to formation becomes a way to satisfy this unrealistic desire for intimacy, much harm can be done, and the capacity to commit oneself can be postponed indefinitely.

These observations and this rather critical, though very brief, examination of the dynamics underlying modern approaches to formation, may come across as negative. I hope that no one will yield to the temptation to say, "Perhaps we should go back to the good old days, with the early hours, long meditations, the rites and rituals of discipline, and the whole clear-cut system of reward and punishment." Before we make that mistake, allow me to raise, by way of conclusion, the question of leadership within the structures of authentic religious community.

First of all, let me note that dialogue and small-group living are both highly sensitive areas of human activity, which require a responsible and competent leader. If it be true that a discussion can unite as well as separate; and if it be true that dialogue can help people to grow up, as well as become the occasion for them to fall apart; and if it also be true that a small group can be task-oriented as well as self-centered, we are involved in a highly important and humanly sensitive area of life, which cannot be left to the processes of trial and error. If no one accepts this responsibility, then emotions, ideas and plans will be like water which is not guided by a river bed but which washes all over the place, destroying land instead of irrigating it. The person who accepts this leadership responsibility should be able to provide creative channels through which life can become both meaningful and purposive. This is why we say that such sensitive processes as dialogue and group living require a well-defined responsibility in order to be effective.

Such responsibility means, certainly among other things, that some form of competent leadership must exist by which structure can be brought to dialogue and group processes. Let me mention just a few of the different ways in which this leadership can function:

a) Good leadership can prevent group processes from becoming amateur forms of group therapy. The expression of love and hate,

anger and frustration, hostility and erotic desires, without special
control, careful supervision and well-defined goals is dangerous
and tends to harm people more than help them;

b) Again, competent leadership can foster at times of crisis the
right atmosphere for discussion of certain existential issues. Such
a discussion can have a temporary value that is very important.
When the leader is not an equal participant, but represents
more than an individual opinion, he can make it clear to those
in the discussion or the group that they are on safe grounds,
protected against dangerous traps;

c) Another function of competent leadership is that it keeps communication in a group free and open. No one can be forced,
nor should be forced to enter a discussion if he does not want it.
Many people either do not have anything to say, or are not yet
ready to say it, and any or several forms of subtle pressure
to participate in a dialogue can take away freedom of persons
to determine their own degree of intimacy, as well as the pace
of growth that is proper to them as the unique persons they are.

All the best research on group dynamics seems to make clear this
essential idea: that discussion and group living can only bring people
closer together, and enable them to grow individually, if they are
already together in some way. As a result good leadership means the
representation of some level of community within which these processes can take place in a healthy and creative way. The leader's
function can be seen as an expression of the authority which belongs
to the community in the first place. The task of the competent leader,
therefore, can be seen as safeguarding the boundaries of the community, and of judging which ideas, feelings and actions can be
handled within these boundaries and which cannot. The persons
taking part in such discussions, or in such living processes, will feel
much freer to express themselves when they know that they will be
warned when they trespass or go astray.

Competence in the role and function of those in charge of the
formation processes, therefore, is an extremely important element in
the formation process itself. It both stimulates and safeguards personal growth, and is able to bring up and cope with even loaded
questions within the healthy context of an authentic religious com-

munity structure. And so, as a final word, I should like to say a few things about religious community.

Religious community is *ecclesia*; it means called out of the land of slavery to the land of the free. It means a constant readiness to move away from the *status quo*, searching for what is beyond the here and now. As soon as any community becomes sedentary, it is tempted to lose its original faith, and worship the wayside gods of the world instead of the One True God who is leading it in a pillar of fire.

So, when we speak about vocation, we must ask first of all whether the community has a vocation that means experiencing itself as being called out of Egypt, the land of depression and stagnation, to a new and as yet undiscovered country. Some communities lose their vital thrust and become so enchanted by the beautiful oasis of existence which they found on their way that they settled for that and forgot their real call.

This is why I think that one of the best ways to look at the vocation of the individual candidate is to see it as a participation in the vocation of the community at large. When many candidates come to the religious life and few of them stay it might very well be due to the fact that they have not been able to find the vocation in which they can participate. If they find a group of people too preoccupied with internal conflicts, wrapped up in small, insignificant debates about rituals, rules and authority and remarkably blind to the fact that most of their energy is expended on trivia while the world is on the verge of committing suicide, they inevitably wonder, and sometimes they do more than wonder; they simply leave. A self-centered community tends to throw the candidate back on herself and encourage her to be over-reflective, suggesting that vocation is an internal inspiration which can be discovered through endless self-scrutiny. The end result of such a situation is that the candidate takes herself much too seriously, and begins to ask her superiors to pay constant attention to her most individual needs and desires.

I think that, quite often, the problem of vocation is not with the candidates. Usually they want to give their best. Nor is the problem entirely with the formation personnel, who are for the most part willing and able to do anything for their candidates. The problem is, rather, with the community at large, which has somehow lost its most basic conviction: that its existence is mandatory because it is called to fulfill a task for Christ in a manner that no one else is able to fulfill it.

There is no lack of generosity. In fact, there is so much of it that the one who can mobilize and channel it can move mountains and make the impossible dream come true. I am convinced that a community which experiences itself as called to a difficult task, which asks for great sacrifices and great self-denial in order to do the work of God which is obviously there and needs to be done, such a community will have few problems in finding people who want to join in the challenging enterprise. The frank promise of hard work, long hours, and much sacrifice will attract the strong and the generous, but the alluring promise of protection, of success, with all the facilities and fatuities of an affluent society will have to settle for the weak, the lazy and the spoiled. It is a sad commentary on our congregations when it is not the weak and lazy who leave our religious communities, but the strong and the generous, who had too much to give to do their best in an easy life.

This is why, in the matter of vocation and religious formation, the religious community as a whole has a task. Its task is to be and to continually become itself, that is to say a sign that is truly the sign of *ecclesia*, constantly resisting the temptation to lose contact with its pillar of fire.

A religious community can only survive when it stays in contact with this fire. It is this same fire which was the symbol of the new community of the people of God on Pentecost. Instead of huddling together and clinging to each other in fear, the apostles opened the doors, stepped out into the world and went where the spirit of God led them. They knew that they were carried and supported by more than the psychological experience of sympathy and friendship.

This is what Jesus indicated to the generous but hard-headed Peter when he asked him three times: "Do you love me more than these others do?" Jesus meant *agape*, not *philia*. It took Peter a while to understand the difference. It takes all of us a while to understand it. But Jesus meant that only this divine love, *agape*, would make it possible for Peter to fulfill his vocation. The reason is simple: a real vocation is a calling out by the spirit which leads us not where we may want to go, but rather where we need to go, and where we would oftentimes not go. The formation process in religious community is meant to provide for, to allow, and to stimulate this growth to that maturity of love, strengthened by the divine love. It is only thus that one comes to understand that the Cross is no longer a sign of failure and indecision, but a sign of commitment and hope.

Consecration for Life

REV. THOMAS E. CLARKE, S.J.
Woodstock College, Woodstock, Maryland

The subject of this paper is consecration for life, and I understand this term in a twofold sense: first, in the sense of a lifetime dedication, a covenant of fidelity with the Lord till the hour of death, and secondly, in the sense of a consecration whose very meaning is life, and not death; enrichment, and not diminishment. I understand this distinction in somewhat the same fashion as the Scripture scholars understand the beautiful opening of chapter 13 of the Gospel according to John: Having loved His own who were in the world, He loved them to the very end of His life. But also: Having loved His own who were in the world, He loved them to the uttermost limits of His love, with deathless love. In the first sense, consecration for life is a question of how long—a question of duration, of quantity. In the second and more profound sense, consecration for life is a question of how deep, a question of intensity, of quality. Both questions are important, and both are difficult. But I will be suggesting that to find any adequate answer at all to the first question we must explore the mystery of the second. I will be suggesting also that our real problem with commitment today is not permanency, but quality and depth. That is why I think the three consensus statements from last summer's workshop on formation have something special to say to us.

Let us begin by examining the first question—permanency. The last few years have raised for American religious men and women a whole series of questions touching the enduring character of the religious consecration, especially as this consecration finds expression in the three traditional vows of religion. It is important, I think, that we distinguish several questions now being asked, some of them far more fundamental than others.

115

First, there is the question whether consecration to the life of the counsels needs to find expression precisely in vows, that is, in promises of a sacred and juridically binding character made to God in the presence of the Church to follow the life of the counsels. Canonically the present law of the Church (Canon 488) considers as religious in the strict sense only those who take vows. Religious Institutes in this strict sense are thus distinct from societies of men and women living a common life without vows. After the promulgation of the code of 1918, the Church recognized secular institutes, so that another kind of evangelical life came into being without the necessity of vows. This canonical distinction, while insisted on in such documents as the recent instruction on the renewal of religious formation, today is widely regarded as of secondary importance. In Vatican II, the decree *Perfectae Caritatis*, even though it mentions the distinction (n. 1) and discusses secular institutes (n. 11), proceeds on the whole, according to a broad sense of "religious," which means, equivalently, "follower of the evangelical counsels in Church communities." The Constitution on the Church, in the charter on the religious life, uses as its central conception the notion of three evangelical counsels, and says explicitly that "the faithful of Christ can bind themselves to the three . . . counsels *either* by vows, *or* by other sacred bonds which are life vows in their purpose" (n. 44).

It is interesting that the proposed norms for the revision of Canon Law submitted by our American Major Superiors of Women, while they do preserve the distinction of religious institutes, societies of common life and secular institutes, do not speak of vows as proper to religious institutes. "Public profession of Christian life in community in the way of the Gospel counsels" is how permanent incorporation is described (n. 48).

Theologically speaking, I would say that the distinction between the three kinds of Church communities following the life of the counsels is of secondary importance. To make too much of this distinction runs today, I believe, the danger either of doing an injustice to the depth of consecration of members of secular institutes and societies of common life, or else the danger, in the name of separation from the world, of keeping apostolic religious women from the kind of life and contact with the world which their mission in the twentieth century calls for. Theologically, too, it is not of primary importance whether one refers to the permanent consecration as vow, promise, commitment, covenant, engagement. It is better to have a promise and keep it well than to have a vow and keep it badly.

A second question: How important is it that there be three vows or promises, and that these three have the names of poverty, chastity and obedience? I would say it is not of primary importance that the formulation of the consecration should be specified in this traditional way; the important thing is that the life itself be chosen and lived, which corresponds to the traditional formula. History, of course, tells us of many changes and developments in the formula of consecration. The tradition of the East, the Benedictine rule, the fact that there was no general vow of obedience till about the ninth century are some illustrations of this. This does not mean, obviously, that the realities designated by poverty, chastity and obedience are not essential to the life of the counsels. It does mean that there are a variety of ways of conceptualizing this evangelical life. For example, one may conceive the celibate Christian community for the sake of the kingdom is the heart of the life, and that poverty, or the sharing of goods, and obedience derive their importance primarily from their value in fostering celibate community.

A third question: What is to be said on the subject of temporary vows? As you know, the recent instruction on formation gives the general chapter, by a two-thirds majority, the power to replace temporary vows with some other kind of commitment. Each community will be deciding whether it wishes to do this. My own feeling is that, whatever the value of temporary vows in the past, they present such difficulties for so many today that, generally speaking, they should be left behind. Undoubtedly different communities, on the basis of experience and reflection, will work out a variety of ways in which a member will be related to the community prior to her definitive commitment, and ways in which such relationships can be formulated and celebrated.

A fourth question concerns the time of life best suited to permanent commitment, and the length of time that should elapse between entrance and permanent commitment. The instruction on formation sets limits of three to nine years from the end of the novitiate. Here again experience and reflection should be the guide. There seems to be a growing consensus that the length of the period should be shaped to the individual, and the time of definitive consecration should be fixed by mutual agreement. There seems likewise to be agreement that, at least in general, definitive engagement in the religious life should be undertaken not before the middle or late twenties. Dr. Joseph English has suggested that the 20-to-30 period in the development of young people be creative and generative, not decisional.[1] This may pose practical problems, for instance, for the ex-nun of 27 or 28 who enters into a rather competitive marriage market. And one wonders about the permanent commitment to marriage which in our society takes place usually at a time when the creative and generative period has hardly begun. In any case, the time to say "forever" and really mean it is the time when a relative maturity has been achieved, the time when a realistic appreciation, based on some appropriate experience of other possible options, makes the decision for this kind of life as fully free as possible.

We begin now to move toward the more basic questions. For example: can the religious life, in its essentials, be lived without a lifetime consecration to it, with the door always open, so to speak? Here again, it is important to keep in mind several distinct questions. I will be arguing later that the life of the counsels, as a distinct Christian life-form, does call for a permanent engagement. But there are several things which this permanent engagement does not exclude: *First*, it does not exclude that we have some groups or communities in the Church, including celibate groups, in which permanency of commitment is not part of the structure, in which the decision to remain celibate for the sake of apostolic work in a particular group will have the nature of a career decision fully open to be changed. *Secondly*, it does not exclude that, within a community whose basic or core membership is committed on the basis of a lifetime dedication, there should also be associate members who never make such a lifetime commitment. In the conditions of life today, there would seem to be a good deal to be said for such communities, which have historical antecedents in such kinds of membership as that of oblates and donnés. A further question here would be whether such associate membership could be extended to married people. The various efforts made at heterogeneous communities (celibates and married) in the past are not entirely encouraging, perhaps, but it may be that we are in a period of the life of the Church and the world where this difficult dream may be capable of achievement. As I understand the Focolare movement, it represents such a heterogeneous grouping of dedicated Christians. I would understand such a conception as in con-

tinuity with the association religious and seculars had in the past
through third Orders, Sodalities and similar groups.

Even if one grants that such heterogeneous groups should now have
a greater place in the Church, there is the further question whether
they should not be, by and large, new groups. We all need to come
closer to married Christians, but this can take place in various ways.
Where the relationship would be so intimate as to involve proper
membership, however, we have to ask whether the consequent adjustment of institutions and mentality would be truly creative or whether
it would be destructive. Not every form of Christian living is for
everyone. Our history provides us with opportunities, but they are
not unlimited. "In My Father's house there are many mansions," and,
thank God, they are not all built to the same blueprint.

The final question is the most fundamental and difficult, and so
I would like to devote most of my time to it. It is the basic question
of the legitimacy and special value of a lifetime consecration to God
and man within the context of a particular celibate community. For
many reasons—psychological, cultural, religious—this is a widespread
doubt which has come into the minds of many today. Let me first
explore some of the reasons for doubting, and then suggest a few
avenues of theological and pastoral reflection.

First, I think our question stems in large part from massive cultural
change. Permanency in the ancient and medieval world was one thing,
permanency in the modern and contemporary context is another. The
cosmos of ancient and medieval man invited men to prize permanency
and stability. The stars were fixed in their places, or at least fixed in
the regular cycle of their predetermined course. Everything had its
natural place in the Aristotelian world, and should it be temporarily
dislodged from that place, it was impelled by inner forces to get back
to where it belonged. Such a view of the cosmos invited men to conceive the human microcosm, both individual and corporate, as being
likewise a very orderly and static process, in which sheer permanency
was to be treasured. Everyone had his place in society, the king, the
nobles, the commoners, the serfs. Economically, society had little mobility: if you were born a serf, chances are you would die a serf.
And in the Church the various orders and states designated where
each person and group belonged.

In such a world, permanency was a prime value. God's eternity
tended to be conceived as the permanency of a God Who never

changed. If man's vocation was to be like God, then permanency was man's destiny, too, and stability in the forms of life the more appropriate way to reach the goal. Human life on earth would thus anticipate and reflect the unending and unchanging peace of the eternal city.

But now much of this has changed. From Darwin to Teilhard we have assimilated into our consciousness the feeling that nothing is permanently itself, that primate gets transformed into man; and man, we suspect, may well be destined for a transfiguration into something or someone we can't as yet imagine. Einstein has taught us that all things are relative. Marx has interpreted history as a dialectic, a struggle in which it is not *just* the same thing over and over again, but a movement to a goal which, though inevitable from one point of view, still has to be created, particularly by an avant-garde, a spearhead group. And Freud has involved us all in the anxious quest for what we really are, for an understanding of what we really meant when we said "Forever," and in the growing doubt that perhaps we really didn't mean it, really didn't say it freely, and that we now have to search elsewhere for our true identity. Kierkegaard has held up to us the ideal of the lonely knight of faith, forever in pursuit of the impossible dream. And currently we all seem to be in the throes of a binge of romanticism, with every man free to do his thing, usually a different thing, and a changing thing. These and many other influences have made our world one in which it is not permanency and stability that are honored, but mobility, process, pluralism of points of view, an accent on contingency, the spirit of search, and the refusal of total commitment lest we be trapped into a sterile and invalid existence. All of these are in the air we breathe today, and our young people have hardly breathed any other air at all. Kenneth Keniston speaks in his study of alienation among the young of "an unwillingness to make commitments that might seem to limit the capacity for experience." [2] In such a world, are perpetual vows not a closing of the door which leads to experience, life, adventure?

To these cultural reasons why permanency is in crisis today we must add some theological and religious ones. Historically it was Luther who challenged the validity of a binding, lifetime consecration by vow, and he did so in the name of the Gospel. Monastic vows, he argued, were an insult to God and man: to God because they were a pretentious effort at justification by works, by human merits, an assault on the freedom of God to bestow his gifts on whom He will; an insult to man because they deprived Christian man of his freedom to respond to the Spirit wherever He might call.

There is in Catholic circles today, a good deal of sympathy with this viewpoint of Luther on permanent vows, as on several other questions. By binding ourselves for life to a particular community, are we not unduly limiting our freedom to follow the call of the Spirit? The development of the theology of marriage and of secular engagement in the world has opened the eyes of many religious to alternative options for dedicated Christians, married or celibate. Especially if our community be reluctant to renew itself, how can there be a responsibility to stay with that foundering and possibly sinking ship till death, when life outside the community beckons us to a richer human and Christian experience, to a freer service of human needs, and perhaps to a more demanding responsibility to God and man?

Sometimes, in response to such objections, appeal is made to the permanency of the marriage covenant. Those who question the value of permanency will answer sometimes in terms of the responsibility for children which is peculiar to the marriage covenant, and sometimes more radically by saying that we have to rethink the permanency of marriage, too.

Finally, where the defenders of permanency stress the incomparable value of an absolute lifetime commitment to God, the doubters will respond that this covenant is not the prerogative of religious but the gift and responsibility of every baptized Christian. A religious who decides, even after many years, to carry out this commitment within marriage is changing only the form of his following of Christ, not the substance. *The* vocation is the baptismal vocation.

Such, in brief, are some of the reasons offered today in what can only be described as a crisis of permanent consecration. When these intellectual arguments are confirmed by the withdrawal from religious life of large numbers of men and women, including some of the most talented, then we are all impelled to ask: what price permanency? Would it not be more Christian and more practical simply to relinquish the mystique of permanency in the religious consecration, make it easier for people to come and go, and assume a much simpler and less idealistic stance toward this form of Christian life?

I have no overall answer to the problem. I would like to suggest some approaches, especially of a theoretical kind, centering on the notion of fidelity. In many ways, the key to the problem of permanency is in the idea and the experience of fidelity, in its psychological, philosophical and theological dimensions.

Fidelity is, first of all, a value and a response consequent upon an experience of another person or of a community, and experience of that person or community in its mystery and in its exigency. At a particular moment of my personal history, my destiny has become intertwined with another destiny, and this moment of epiphany, of revelation, has brought into my life a joyful but compelling necessity which was not there before. *I can do no other*—this is the way Fr. Schillebeeckx expresses it. Not that I am not free to choose, either initially or afterwards. I can do no other, however, in the sense that once I have incorporated this meeting with the other into my way of identifying myself, I cut off, in some genuine sense, the possibility of living my life otherwise than as a response to this person or community.

This moment of discovery and my commitment to let it shape my life finds expression in the word, the promise, the vow. I am yours—you can depend on me—I will be there—I will be true to thee till death. And with the word, the pledge, the vow, the other person or the community can likewise let this moment of encounter shape its life. To the extent to which he trusts me and believes in my fidelity, he can make demands, and he can face his own future in hope because now it is a shared future.

I have given my word and I cannot take it back. Fidelity therefore has in it the quality of being closed, definite, once for all. Each word of ours has so many syllables, so many particular sounds, so many letters. So too the pledged word gives to fidelity an element of stability and permanence. I have paid my vow to the Lord and I cannot take it back. But the mystery of fidelity has in it also the opposite quality of being open. It is related to the unknown future as well as to the clear and definite past. Fidelity would be a mere pragmatic contract fulfillment if we knew fully in advance what it demands. When we give our word to another person or community we are not making a cautious contract hedged in with safeguards and escape clauses. Rather we are saying, "I will be there no matter what." We are saying, "I take you for better or for worse, for richer or for poorer, in sickness and in health, until death."

And so fidelity is a paradox of the closed and the open, the fixed and definite and the indefinable. It points to the past but also to the future. Theologically, the mystery of Christian fidelity is rooted in the mystery of God, Who speaks His Word and breathes forth His Spirit—His once-for-all Word, which stands forever, in Jesus Christ, the living Word of the Lord—and His Holy Spirit, Who is love and breath and wind and fire, Who comes from God only knows where and leads to God only knows where. In proportion as we share life with Father, Son and Spirit, we shall come to understand the meaning of Christian fidelity—and vice versa: living the mystery of Christian fidelity plunges us more and more into the mystery of Father, Son and Spirit.

Into every commitment of Christian fidelity must enter the note of *forever*, the quality of deathlessness. We can, of course, speak of fidelity to a promise to do something that is temporary—to make a pilgrimage or a novena. But when there is question of a basic life-option, of a profound reorientation of our life, as in marriage or consecration to God in celibate community, some element of the "forever" must be present, if we are to respect the meaning of such options. We are not talking about a mere career decision, not even a very important one; such decisions fall short of the kind of dedication envisaged by Christ and the Church in the call to follow the evangelical counsels. Here I have two observations to make:

1) When a man says "forever" or "till death" as he engages himself in fidelity, he is not saying: "for a very long time." The "forever" is merely a very imperfect expression of the *depth*, the *quality* of his engagement. There is no special value in duration as such; it is valuable only to the extent to which it expresses or confirms the element of depth, intensity, quality in our love. Fifty years in the religious life are not necessarily of more value than five years. A person who engages himself for one year with intensity and then dies or leaves for good reason has been far more faithful than someone who just sticks it out superficially for fifty or sixty years.

2) When a person says "till death" when he consecrates himself to God, he is not merely indicating the expiration date of a contract. He is rather prefiguring the event of his death in Christ as the consummation of his lifelong consecration. He wants so to live, so to anticipate that supreme moment, that it will be the most perfect act of covenant love. That is why he is willing, under vow, to live each

day a death to some of life's most cherished values, so that his death itself, when it comes, may be the most perfect consecration for life. I do not think we can adequately appreciate Christian fidelity, or the meaning of a vowed existence, unless we relate it to death in Christ, in baptism, in daily Christian existence, and in the moment of passage from this world to the Father.

And so, I suggest, if there is a crisis regarding permanency in religious life today, it is ultimately a crisis of depth, a crisis of the quality of the commitment both in its initial moment and subsequently. Recently I heard a psychiatrist familiar with the religious life quoted as saying that, while we have taken steps to see that only well balanced people will enter religious life, we now need to be concerned lest we end up with superficial people, people without depth. Bernard Lonergan, in speaking of the capacity for autonomy as characteristic of the adult, writes very perceptively about the opposite quality:[3]

> The opposite to this open-eyed, deliberate self-control is drifting. The drifter has not yet found himself; he has not yet discovered his own deed and so is content to do what everyone else is doing; he has not yet discovered his own will and so he is content to choose what everyone else is choosing; he has not yet discovered a mind of his own and so he is content to think and say what everyone else is thinking and saying; and the others too are apt to be drifters, each of them doing and choosing and thinking and saying what others happen to be doing, choosing, thinking, saying.

From Bernard Lonergan to the Beatles is quite a jump, but the Beatles, too, in their own inimitable way, have said (or sung) the same thing in their ballad, "Nowhere Man."

At this point it would be quite comforting, for some of us at least, to use the idea of drifting of the "Nowhere Man," to explain the large-scale departures from the religious life. Undoubtedly some who are leaving are people without depth who in the pre-Vatican II Church were protected in their religious life by a favorable climate, stable structures, uniformity and regularity, etc., but who now, in the new climate, find themselves without adequate personal resources to survive in the new and very exposed kind of existence. But this is only one aspect of the total picture. I would suggest that when there is a question of fidelity, of the depth and quality of consecration, in contrast to the spirit of drifting, we should ask the question also about our communities and about those who remain, and not only about those who leave. Could it possibly be that the reason why some individuals are leaving, individuals whose fidelity to Christ does have this quality of depth, is that their communities have substituted for genuine fidelity a dead conformity to the past, and, despite superficial reforms, are unable or unwilling to grow up in Christ, and so go on drifting and dreaming without substantive renewal?

What I am suggesting here is that the crisis of permanency is really a crisis of depth, a crisis of the quality of our covenant with the Lord. And if we wish really to come to terms with the problem of permanency, then all of us, individuals and communities, must face squarely the attitudes and conditions which make us drifters instead of deeply committed Christians. Let us ask not only, "Are these *individuals* capable of a life-time commitment?" Let us ask also: "Is this *community* able and willing to commit itself in covenant with the Lord unto death, i.e. with a depth and quality of commitment which corresponds to the depth and quality of the Spirit's call?" And am *I* able and willing for this *kind* of commitment? "Having loved His own who were in the world, He loved them to the uttermost limits of His love."

Mentioning the community in connection with fidelity prompts this further reflection: The covenant we make in the religious profession is a covenant with man and not only with God. When I say in the moment of ratifying this covenant, "I am yours," "I will be there," "You can depend on me," I am saying it to the members of my community (and more broadly to the whole Church and all mankind), and my community in turn is saying it to me. The day of religious profession is a day on which the community, along with its new members professes its allegiance, its fidelity. On each profession day the whole community stands at the foot of Sinai, in the Temple, on Calvary, in a moment of covenant renewal. This means, for example, that when an individual religious comes into a period of crisis and begins to re-examine her covenant—something which she not only may but sometimes must do—she has to ask herself not only, "How am I now to be faithful to my word pledged to the Lord?" but also, "How am I now to be faithful to my word pledged to my sisters and to the Church?" I have told them as well as the Lord:

"You can depend on me," and I must keep my word. This does not mean, of course, that fidelity will always keep a person in the community; it may in fact sometimes command that she leave. But the decision to leave, like the decision to enter must be a decision taken, in some fashion, in the presence of the community, and not in isolation from it. And the community on its part must be concerned for its own fidelity to this individual member, not only in her entering and preserving but also in her going, and, I would be inclined to say, after her departure.

But I have not yet touched on the most difficult aspect of our problem. What of the view that the only absolute commitment for a Christian is the one he makes at baptism, and that any further commitment must have a tentative character? I don't see how one can simply deny this. The basic consecration of every Christian is to love without limit, to follow the Spirit wherever He leads. And no Christian can have an absolute guarantee that God's baptismal call to him will continue till death to be a call to fulfill his baptismal promises within a celibate Christian community. To this extent Luther was right.

On the other hand, we cannot reduce the consecration to the life of the counsels merely to an important career decision which may be reversed with relative ease. The basic fact, verifiable in 2,000 years of Christian history, is that Christ, Who comes into the life of all Christians in varying degrees, comes into the life of some Christians in a distinctive way. It may be that, as Brother Rast and others think, these are people psychologically disposed for this special kind of call, that they are people whose revelatory experience with the mystery of life and death compels them to incorporate that mystery not only into their attitudes and responses to life but into the very structure of their life. From this point of view, celibacy, poverty, obedience are three exclamation points placed after the name of Christ Jesus at the head of the *curriculum vitae* of these Christians; they are a cry—at once a warning and an invitation and a song and a protest and a laugh —a cry addressed to anyone willing to open his ears, but also a cry that doesn't care whether anyone is listening at the moment or not, a cry which proclaims "We shall overcome," which challenges "Come to where the real flavor is," which invites, "Lift up your hearts."

Only love is credible, says Hans Urs von Balthasar, and this bridging of the credibility gap in contemporary life must be written not only into the substance of Christian living but into its form, and this particular form of Christian living, the life of the counsels, unlike other forms, is itself incredible except there is love. And I mean not merely, "Except there is human love, except human beings care for one another." I mean, "Except there be, at the very bottom of human life, underneath the pain and the pleasure, the discovery and the bafflement, the great hopes and the little despairs, at the very well springs of life, a love which surpasses all understanding, and which we call God." Only love is credible, but perhaps this divine love, being so profound and hidden, needs itself to be rendered credible, by the lives of those who believe that the first and the last word is God Who is love; and perhaps this rendering of love credible, which is the work of faith, requires that in some Christian lives, at least, there be an unambiguous witness that it is love—divine love—that makes the world go round. To attach a date of expiration to such a witness, or to put it in the category of a career choice, seems absurd. And once again, the issue is not permanency but quality: what *kind* of a choice is the religious profession? If it is a choice in depth, a quality choice, if it is a congruous response of fidelity to Him whose great love is without end, then it is hard to view it except as qualitatively different from ordinary career decisions.

I have no illusions about having plumbed the depths of explanation of the mystery of consecration for life, or about having answered the many difficulties, theoretical and practical, surrounding this mystery. What I have said may, however, enable us to say something about these difficulties. For example: the fidelity involved in consecration for life in the qualitative sense is not to be identified with the medieval prizing of permanency as such. Here let me refer to the pages in Sister Helen Marie Beha's book on the meaning of fidelity to commitment, and how it differs from mere constancy.[4]

What I have said may help, too, in understanding and evaluating departures from religious life. When the crisis arises, there are many questions which must be faced: Did the individual ever really make a permanent commitment in the qualitative sense? Did she enter a community which was itself able and willing to live at this intensity of life? Where the original commitment was truly free, we must try to see to it that, in the hour of crisis, the individual religious realizes that her commitment made her responsible to a community, and that the community now must enter into her reevaluation of commitment. We must try to see to it also that, as her original commitment was a loving response to the undying fidelity of God Who is love, so now no change in the form of her life will take place except as a generous and discerning response to a relatively clear call of that same undying fidelity. And finally, because only God knows the hearts of men, both those who stay and sometimes appear mediocre, and those who leave and sometimes appear flighty or unfaithful, must remain for us what they are, our brothers and sisters, who need our compassion, and whose compassion we need.

Though I have not made this long discussion a direct commentary on the three consensus statements of the 1968 workshop at Woodstock, I think I have been indirectly contributing to our understanding of them. If our real problem is not permanency as such but the quality of our commitment and the depth of our fidelity, then I see each of the three papers—on prayer and spiritual direction, on person and community, on incorporation into the community—as three challenges to enter into a genuine renewal in depth and in quality. If we are men and women of prayer, free to live as genuine Christian persons in genuine Christian community, and if the forms and spirit of incorporating new members prepare us to be that kind of people, we will have come a long way to meet our present crisis. And we will understand as never before just what it means to be—consecrated for life.

In summary and conclusion, then: what is the meaning of consecration for life, fidelity unto death, in following the life of the counsels? What is its value and its justification? Here are some of the things we can say about it, and say for it:

There are some people who find no other way of expressing and responding to the incredible love of God for men, and to the deathless fidelity of Jesus Christ to His beloved, the Church, except by writing the word "forever" with their own blood into the very shape and structure of their lives.

There are some people whom God calls to the gamble of faith, as Fr. Donald Heintschl has expressed it (and that word can also be spelled "gambol" and still be accurate and significant), because He asks them to entrust their weakness, their stupidity, to the weakness and stupidity of others like themselves, so that when the miracle of reconciliation and joy in community takes place, there can be no explanation except that the power and wisdom of God has appeared among us.

And there are some people whom God asks to make manifest in their life-style that human life is for pilgrimage and not for drifting; that our destiny is not to be "nowhere men" and "nowhere women" but a pilgrim people with roots in the City of God; that it is the quality and depth of human life which counts, and not the number of years we live on this earth; and that the only congruous response for the gift of freedom is to give it back wholly to God, freedom's self and freedom's giver, without even the possibility, so far as in us lies, of ever again being free apart from Him.

There are indeed such people, and we who are here today are those people. If we glory in it—and I think we should—we do so not as some kind of elite—God knows we are not an elite—but, like Paul, we glory that the power and wisdom of God has chosen our particular weakness and our unique stupidity to manifest itself to men, for the praise and glory of His grace.

Does consecration for life in the way of the counsels have anything to say to contemporary man? Does contemporary man need a witness to fidelity? Does he need a reminder that his precious years on earth are given not for drifting but for pilgrimage? Does he need help to keep him from being a cipher, an anonymity, a "nowhere man"? Does he need to be called back to a taste and a yearning for quality and depth in human life? Can he be helped by seeing weak and foolish people like himself so willing to trust one another that they have promised one another to remain together until death? And does someone—perhaps relatively few, but still someone—need to keep alive in the heart of contemporary man the embattled hope that behind the absurdity there is ultimate meaning, and beneath the carnage of death there is life, and that at the very end of the human pilgrimage there stands, still unseen and unheard, that one uncritical lover of man, that Father Who entrusted His own Son to our human keeping, that Father Who in Jesus Christ has loved us to the uttermost limits of His love?

Franz Kafka left behind him, among his unfinished fragments, the vision of a vast city at night in which just a few people are awake. And he compared it to a military encampment in which everyone is asleep except a few guards on the battlements, keeping watch. And he asks why these few are awake when the rest are asleep. And he answers: "Because someone must be watching—someone must be there."

Perhaps, ultimately, this is all we can really say about ourselves when we speak of lifetime consecration; this is really all we can say about why we are here, in this stubborn and mischievous kind of life: because *someone* must be watching—*someone* must be there.

NOTES

1. *Celibacy: The Necessary Option*, ed. G. Frein (New York, 1968), p. 157.

2. *The Uncommitted* (New York, 1965), p. 192.

3. "Existenz and Aggiornamento," *Collection* (New York, 1967), p. 242.

4. *Living Community* (Milwaukee, 1967), pp. 32–49.

Service, Eschatology, and the Religious Life

Rev. Christian Ceroke, o.c.d.
The Catholic University of America, Washington, D.C.

It has been said that religious life is one of the most significant barometers that takes the measure of the life of the Church. Of all the Church's sub-institutions religious life, since it lies so close both to the gospel and to the magisterium, is more apt to be sensitive to the issues affecting the Church and the more apt to react vigorously to attempted solutions to these issues.

As if to verify the barometer theory, religious life since Vatican II has been subjected to serious, if not profound, re-evaluation. Undoubtedly, much that was said by the Fathers of the Council struck resonant chords in the hearts of multitudes of men and women in religious life. Change and renewal have been taken seriously, if not always with the same degree of enthusiasm or from similar standpoints, by both older and younger members of religious communities.

Numerous meetings, efforts at dialogue, position papers, and chapters have succeeded in effecting both change and renewal, although to a degree that does not admit of easy analysis. Yet it is fair to say that religious life still seeks that degree and type of change and renewal that will best accord with the demands of living the gospel. It cannot be said that religious are as yet satisfied that the vision and program of Vatican II have been effectively implemented. Indeed, it is not entirely clear what constitutes in practice a truly accurate implementation in the religious life of the guidelines of Vatican II. Significant and even radical changes in the structure of daily existence, in lifestyle including dress, which were necessary or useful for up-dating, have certainly provided many religious with a greater sense of per-

131

tinence to the world in which they live and work. Yet these changes
have also occasioned more profound, not to say nagging questions
that provoke a spiritual uneasiness in many religious.

Paradoxically, while the changes brought about to date have enabled
religious to perform more comfortably as part of the real world, they
have also tended to blur the sense of personal identity that in the past
so forcefully and clearly accompanied membership in a religious order or congregation. A religious professionally trained to teach or to
perform professional services in the medical or social fields is faced
with the question of the differentiation between himself and the professional laity who serve in the same capacities. Obviously, it is not
the value of the work performed that differentiates the religious professional from the lay professional. Nor is it the disposition of the
financial remuneration from such work that constitutes a significant
difference between them. The lay person is inclined to envy the religious his "security" on the ground that without personal responsibility
for a household the religious is simply free of such responsible concerns altogether. The religious may be amused by such naiveté when
he surveys the complexity of responsibilities his community and its
members inherited from past administrative decision-making, or he
may be annoyed by the implication that he sought out, or remains
in, religious life to escape the burdens of the lay life. On the contrary, many have left the religious life with the conviction that the
burdens of the lay life will be no more challenging, and may in fact
be less so, than those they have encountered in religious life. Whatever the variety of reasons occasioning departures from the religious
life in recent years, they certainly have nothing to do with the relative ease or hardship of the religious versus the lay life.

Religious do not evaluate their lives in terms of burdens undertaken
or escaped from, but in terms of the meaning of their life-style for
the up-building of the Church. Prior to Vatican II the meaning of
religious life was thought to derive principally from a tradition that
had been proved fruitful and effective for the Church. This tradition
was embodied in the rule and constitutions and also in particular
apostolates. Since Vatican II certain guiding ideas in modern religious
thought have taken precedence over the old tradition as the source
for the value-judgment on religious life. These ideas, which lie also
behind the formulations of Vatican II, are embodied chiefly in the

notion of secularization with its emphasis on personalism, freedom, community and education.

Applied to religious life the theory is that the process of secularization will succeed in fashioning religious communities that will find a fruitful and effective place in a world concerned with the values of the secular. Yet this very secularization process has also raised the question whether religious life is necessary at all in a world of the secular, since it appears that what the individual religious can achieve as a member of the secularization process he can also achieve as a lay person.

Due to the effort to assess the value of religious life on a standard that embraces also secular values, without abandoning the old tradition of the spirit of the rule, religious life has been more and more pressingly confronted with the question of its survival within the secular: how can religious life confront the secular, be a real part of the secular, even measure its values by the secular, and yet maintain itself as a sub-institution in the Church with a unique and fruitful meaning?

One source for reflection on religious life and the secularization process is the New Testament record of the lives of St. Paul and of Jesus himself. Their views on life and their method of living it share in the characteristics that distinguish the secular outlook. This frame of mind may be described as possessing four distinguishing features: 1) it is chiefly concerned with the temporal, *the now*, rather than with a future world to come; 2) it is mainly preoccupied with the daily activities that are of concrete service to the needs of one's neighbor by comparison with participation in strictly religious activities; 3) it is interested in knowledge and learning that derive from human effort and empirical methods, and is unwilling to be totally guided by what is thought to be the norm of faith; 4) it has a special concern for human autonomy, that is, that the human person be freed of every unreasonable domination from outside himself, so that he can truly become himself.

If these characteristics of the secular mentality be pushed to an extreme, they inevitably lead to the destruction of Christian faith; for they then become the "secularist" mentality, which denies any life beyond this one, repudiates man's need for worship, rejects all knowledge except that gained from laboratory experiment or the observation of nature in action, and which acknowledges no law above man than man himself (cf. the analysis of the secular outlook in John MacQuarrie, *God and Secularity* [1967], 45–49). Today's Christian secularity is an attempt to incorporate human cultural concerns with the temporal, with the daily activities of human existence, with the quest for knowledge, and with the search for freedom, into the ambit of the gospel. Should religious life succeed in this endeavor, it will undoubtedly find a natural place in a secular world and become a highly effective force for the up-building of the Church.

Yet not a few religious have misgivings over the eventual success of the endeavor. For them the introduction of even a Christian secularity into religious life is destructive of the very reason for its existence: it is a *religious* life, where the Christian faith not only motivates every action, but circumscribes and embraces the whole of life with acts that are openly religious. To de-structure religious life by reducing the *horarium* to a minimum, by making meditation a flexible enterprise, and by conceding a degree of importance to community meetings that approximates the significance of the eucharistic liturgy, is in their view to empty religious life of key realities necessary to its uniqueness.

Religious who entertain no doubts over the necessity and value of Christian secularity find their initial perplexities arising, not over the religious life and the secular, but over the eschatological orientation of the gospel. Is it necessary to be concerned about the meaning of the future when one is well satisfied with grappling with the sense of the present? Does not faith in future realities of heaven, hell, the judgment, and the *parousia* of Christ distract from the present and prevent the religious from becoming a truly adequate secular person? The future can be left to take care of itself; the relevant Christian should concentrate on the present in all things, including prayer.

The student of the New Testament well knows, however, that to de-eschatologize the Gospel is to divest it of its real source of power. To live a life of Christian secularity that is oblivious of the eschatological meaning of Christ is inevitably to become an advocate, not of secularity, but of secularism. Biblical eschatology is not simply future reality; it includes the present activity of God that moves toward the final culmination. The Christian's present relationship to Christ is produced in him for the sake of his future relationship to Christ. Without the Christian future, the present cannot be Christian.

Without hope there cannot be faith. "Now faith is the assurance of things hoped for, the conviction of things not seen" (*Heb* 11: 1). The nature of faith is to place hope in the intangible that is one day to become the reality. Christian hope exists, not because of the Christ of the future, but because the Christ, who is now present *is* the Christ of the future. It is possible to have a truly Christian secularity only on the supposition of the eschatologically present Christ. The Christian, and the religious in particular, is most free to serve the secular when he is most conscious that the meaning of his involvement in the secular derives its force and power from the future reign of Christ that already has its beginning in the present.

That eschatological awareness is a necessary ingredient of Christian secularity is plain from the thought of both Jesus and Paul. Although each of them worked in cultures that were predominantly religious, the characteristics of Christian secularity shine through their lives and work. Jesus took over the traditional Jewish notion of the Kingdom of God, i.e., God's sovereign reign, but, in contrast to the thought of his contemporaries which held it to be a future realization of one final mighty act of God, he declared it to be in existence *now* (*Mk* 1: 14–15). The reign began with a reconstruction of the temporal religious order in Judaism in which people themselves were to share. Jesus' primary concern was neither with the past nor the future, but with a creative renewal of the present. His complaint was that people refused to take responsibility for the necessary changes in their temporal existence (*Mt* 11: 20–24); they preferred to leave the new creation simply to the activity of God (*Mk* 8: 11–12; *Lk* 17: 20). His cleansing of the temple was a symbolic protest against the refusal of the religious authorities to recognize that a new and unique prophetic voice was abroad in the land demanding action *now*. Action was required by the fact that the future reign of God was already begun in the present (cf. Mt's parable of the weeds among the wheat, 13: 24–30).

St. Paul likewise was vitally concerned with the present: "Behold, now is the acceptable time; behold, now is the day of salvation" (2 *Cor* 6:2). Because Paul was aware that the power of Christ actually operated with the Christian (cf. *Gal* 2: 20), he could write to the Colossians, "And whatever you do, in word or in work, do everything in the name of the Lord Jesus, giving thanks to God the Father through him . . ." The presence of Christ in the Christian led the apostle to perceive no essential difference between the holy and the secular in Christian living. The faith-life of the Christian was sufficient to sanctify the created world. But such was true only because the process of resurrection was already begun in the baptized (cf. *Rom* 6: 1–11) and had its effect on creation itself (*Rom* 8: 18–23), which yearned, as it were, for its full sanctification through the revelation of man's full redemption.

This eschatological awareness that attached deep religious significance to the present as an on-going process that led to God enabled both Jesus and Paul to immerse themselves in the affairs of their neighbors without qualms of conscience. Jesus' relatives thought him mad because of his yielding to the demands of people (*Mk* 3: 31), while Paul thought no personal sacrifice of time, food, clothing, or misunderstanding too great to bear for the sake of the gospel (1 *Cor* 5: 9–13; 2 *Cor* 11: 21–29).

Both Jesus and Paul were interested in contemporary evaluations of human life. For them this approach did not mean that the past was irrelevant—far from it, but it did mean that what God was revealing in the present, up-dated the past. The wisdom of the ancients was to be seen in a new light, as Jesus emphasized in the Sermon on the Mount; and whatever could not withstand the scrutiny of the new religious spirit, such as the human religious traditions of the Jews, was to be set aside (*Mk* 7: 1–23). Paul, of course, applied this viewpoint of Jesus rigorously in his letters to the Galatians and Romans, wherein he insisted that rules, regulations, and even commandments were to be understood in the light of saving faith, not as the source of salvation itself. Paul held to this position in spite of being termed antinomian and a renegade from the law and the prophets. For it was *a new spirit* that he perceived was at the heart of Jesus' teaching, and not a simple repudiation of the religious institutions and values of the past.

The fourth characteristic of the secular outlook, concern for human autonomy, was also shared by Jesus and Paul. Jesus rejected the stifling regulations concerning the Sabbath so that people might be free to show their neighborly love for one another. Likewise he voided regulations that subordinated the well-being of people to trifling interpretations of law (cf. *Mk* 2: 23–28). Paul's concern for a human freedom that would enable people to be their better selves is most practically shown in his famous letter to Philemon, in which he uses every possible ploy to convince Philemon to accept Onesimus, not as his escaped slave, but as a Christian man.

Had Jesus and Paul lived in our day the secular outlook would hardly have been alien to their points of view. They would have been concerned with the world as it is now; they would have worked tirelessly to supply the needs of modern man; they would have been eager to inform themselves from modern methods of learning, accepting change as a matter of course; and they would have been sympathetic with every human drive to remove the shackles from legitimate and fruitful autonomy. But because neither of them derived his complete meaning as a person from immersion in the secular, each was ready to accept defeat and even repudiation as also a meaningful part of existence. Jesus accepted the cross, Paul a martyrdom so lonely that only the vaguest details of it have been conserved in historical memory.

If religious life lies at the heart of the gospel, it cannot divorce itself from the eschatological outlook that was the most noteworthy characteristic of Jesus and Paul. It was not their immersion in the secular that caused their lives and ideas to be conserved in the corpus of the New Testament. Many religious thinkers and philosophers have taught ideas similar to theirs. It was their absolute conviction that the future reign of God was what actually appeared as present through their immersion in the secular. To draw this conclusion is not to say that religious life is justified before the world as "an eschatological sign." It is to say rather that religious life is justified in so far as it lives out the gospel, which includes the mystifying paradox that "unless a grain of wheat falls into the earth and dies, it remains alone; but if it dies, it bears much fruit" (*Jn* 12: 24).

The Religious Woman, God, and the World

REV. ERNEST E. LARKIN, O.CARM.
The Catholic University of America, Washington, D.C.

There is no question but that religious life today is going through a period of transition. We may well ask: How is the process faring? It is difficult to say. Communities are at different stages of renovation, and evaluations vary. Many, however, sense something of an impasse at the present moment. There have been many changes in religious life, but where is it all going? Some think the changes are destroying religious life, others that there has been no real change at all. Bells have been dropped, horaria humanized, habits altered, even put aside in favor of secular dress. But has radical renewal taken place? Are religious vibrant, joyful, Easter people, loving communities of dedicated Christians? Or is it another case of the French proverb: "The more the changes, the more things are like themselves"?

The changes so far have had to do mostly with structures. But can religious life be renewed from the outside in? Or must we not follow the Gospel principle of *metanoia*, which is conversion from the inside out? The answer is that we need both a new heart and spirit, "interior renewal," as well as the new structures that are gradually and sometimes painfully being worked out in contemporary religious life. The structures are the vehicle and incarnation of the spirit. Some of them are peripheral, others are creating new life-styles in community and in the apostolate, not only in government, the exercise of authority and obedience, forms of poverty and the common life, but in the most basic values of religious life, which are prayer and community. For a New Pentecost in religious life we need a revitalized faith, hope,

138

and charity and structural reforms imaginative and creative enough to express this new life in the culture of the 1970s.

It is not enough, therefore, to humanize, socialize and secularize the religious life. These things we must do to be part of our times. So we are increasing the opportunities for individuals to grow as authentic persons; we are changing patterns of common observance, so that communities can be communions of friendship and love; we are reforming our apostolates, so that the works are worth doing, real contributions to building up the new earth. But we must do all this in such a way that it is God's work as well as our own.

Replacing the obsolete and the obsolescent, getting rid of irrelevancies and hang-ups from the past, making religious life more human, and therefore, more Christian, bringing convent life into tune with the space age—all that is part of renewal, with a proviso. The proviso is that the reforms are the work of the Holy Spirit. This is not pietism. It is Gamaliel's principle: "If this plan or work is of men, it will be overthrown; but if it is of God, it will last" (cf *Acts 5: 38–39*).

External reforms without the new spirit do not renovate the Church or religious life. Here is a test case. What do you think of these words that appeared recently in a column in the Catholic Press: "Every priest who marries without 'permission' represents a victory for the reform movement. Every seminarian who leaves the seminary in protest against an antiquated clerical life represents a reform triumph." At best, statements like this are equivocal. Opting out may be the answer in given cases, but only if "it seem good to the Holy Spirit and to us" (cf. *Acts 15: 28*), only if a formed Christian conscience dictates this extreme remedy. Otherwise we are truly substituting man-made religion for divinely guided faith. The presumption is against "copping out," as Bishop Butler of England stated eloquently in a recent interview. He urged Catholics to stay in the structures and work for renewal from within with courage and patience and co-responsibility. My point here, however, is not to take a stand against protest or revolt, but to insist that every decision to make changes, especially disruptive ones, must be carefully measured by a higher law and validated in the Holy Spirit. We need discernment of spirits today as never before in the past, for without the Holy Spirit there is no true reform in the Church.

This reflection may sound namby-pamby, as if to take the renewal out of our own hands and to return us to the unquestioning, often naive, and sometimes even magical thinking of pre-Vatican II days. The fact is that renewal is both spiritual and juridical, divine and human. Without the Spirit external changes will be as dead a letter as the evils the reforms are supposed to correct. Spiritual renewal means renewal that is Spirited, Holy-Spirited, changes and reforms that are enlivened and directed by the Holy Spirit. Unless the Holy Spirit re-creates, re-fashions and re-forms both the people and their institutions, our efforts at *aggiornamento* will be not only ineffectual but destructive.

At the end of the Uppsala World Council of Churches meetings (1968), the following evaluation was made by one of the youth representatives: "Renewal," he wrote, "will not come from youth; it can only come from the living God. A new encounter with the living God is a desperate need for all within the Church, for youth as much as for the old." We say with equal conviction: religious renewal will not come from religious; it can only come from the living God.

Changes in structure without change of heart are the adaptations without renewal of which *Perfectae Caritatis* states: ". . . even the most desirable changes made on behalf of contemporary needs will fail of their purpose unless a renewal of Spirit gives life to them." (2,e) Adjustments without renewal are non-salvific. Interior renewal, on the other hand, is always salvific. Inevitably it puts new life into dead bones of archaic institutions and creates new forms. A renewed spirit is the new wine of the Gospels that bursts through the wornout wineskins of the old structures and demands new skins to keep it.

We cannot use the Holy Spirit's role as an excuse for inaction, for do-nothingism. We can be sympathetic with those who are threatened by the erosion of religious practices and structures that served so well even in the recent past. But let the dead bury their dead. The living must move forward, eyes straight ahead, without regrets, even if there is a touch of sadness for what must pass. New ways of living and doing must incarnate the ancient values of religious life in our contemporary culture. New forms will rise out of the ashes of the old, and our only concern must be to search out the values and their appropriate manifestations for our time. This is to listen to the Spirit. He speaks, not in voices from heaven, but in human ideals and secular hopes. These are today's signs of the times.

There is no dichotomy, then, between spiritual renewal and exterior changes. There is no room for two camps among us, one of "spiritualists," the other "structuralists." We must not fall into the error of pushing the reform of structures to the neglect of renewal of spirit, as if the spirit is a private affair and really has nothing to do with practical matters. At the same time we cannot promote renewal of spirit in a vacuum, as if a good retreat would solve the ills which assail religious life today. Spirit and structures go hand in hand; they rise and fall together. They do not represent two approaches to the same one goal; they are one approach, or else no approach at all. They are not separate compartments, but like soul and body, they interpenetrate each other. One is interior to the other. Neither stands alone. While we can conceive our task as beginning with the spirit, we must remember that the spirit cannot survive among men if it is not quickly incarnated in tangible forms and deeds. We can live with abuses, in a state of contradiction, for a while, but only for a while. Either the spirit or the contradiction will give way.

Some documents of Vatican II tend to highlight the distinctions and antitheses in Christian life rather than its unity. The antitheses in question correspond roughly to spirit and structures, to the divine and the human elements in Christianity. According to the *Constitution on the Sacred Liturgy*, for example, the Church is

both human and divine, visible and yet invisibly endowed, eager to act and yet devoted to contemplation, present in the world and yet not at home in it. She is all these things in such a way that in her the human is directed and subordinated to the divine, the visible likewise to the invisible, action to contemplation, and this present world to that city yet to come . . . [n. 2, pp. 137–138 in *The Documents of Vatican II*].

Perfectae Caritatis describes religious life in a series of contrasting doublets that play on its different aspects. Generally the dialectic is being and doing. Thus religious life is both a state of being and a function, a witness and a mission; it is a consecration to God and service to men, at once contemplative and apostolic. These elements describe two movements, one vertical, moving upward toward God, the other horizontal, moving outward toward men. The person who stands at the intersection of these pulls is bound to experience the tension between heaven and earth.

These clear distinctions underline the double vocation of the Chris-

tian and the religious. He must love God and he must love his neighbor. United to God in spirit, he carries out in the structures and patterns of daily existence the demands of faith, hope, and charity. On
the basis of the double movement we can develop a valid philosophy
of religious life. The religious woman stands at the crossroads, looking up to God and looking out into the world. Her life is a search for
union with God and for community with her fellowmen. Prayer is
her vertical occupation, fraternal charity and the apostolate the horizontal obligation. There is no danger of confusing these two. God is
not people, nor are people God. Love of God is not love of neighbor,
nor is prayer identified with building community or promoting human
values. Life is a rhythmic movement from one to the other of these
two occupations: now one prays, now he works, now he prays again.
Priority is given to prayer; community is the effect of prayer, and
structures grow out of union with God.

This summary, brief and partial as it is, seems to characterize the
"old spirituality." The old spirituality nourished countless souls in the
past, and still has much to recommend it. It is valid. But is it viable
today? Does it not run counter to contemporary religious culture?
Today's generation is impatient with distinctions that separate instead
of unifying human life. Life is experienced today as moving in one
direction, at once forward and toward God. Thus the religious woman
of today would see herself as a person living in community, and her
whole life, this life with others in the world, is God-oriented. She
seeks a different image or diagram to illustrate her relationships with
God and the world.

One possible image is three concentric circles. The center circle is
Christ, the sacrament and revelation of the Father. The middle circle
represents the world; it stands for people, the cosmos, for individuals
and communities, for the "you's" in my life. The outer circle is the
religious woman herself, the person, the "I." The rings are not stand-
ing still; they vibrate into each other, now from the center outwards,
now from without to within. They interpenetrate one another. The
two outer rings represent the human side, the structures of religious
life. The center ring is the spirit. Christian life is a constant interaction
between the center and the two outside rings, between spirit and
structures. The diagram shows that life with each other and with
Christ is one.

A man's life is lived in the outer rings, but with power from the center. He does not live in isolation on the outer ring, not at least if he has a human existence. He is defined as a person by the persons in his life. "You" make me what I am; you give me meaning and value, because I make a difference to you. Without you I cannot be; but in communion with you I grow, as indeed do you in our mutual love. Christ enters my life through you. He enters these outer rings as the ultimate You in our life, the One who gives me and you ultimate meaning. He calls us together in Himself; He speaks to us in the I-You condition of human existence. I become a Christian when I recognize Him as the center of my life.

I recognize the *Christus praesens* in faith. He is the Risen Lord, who speaks to me through His Spirit, especially in the people in my life. This means that He speaks to me in the cosmos, in history, as well as in Word and Sacrament. Contemporary theology locates Christ where he promised to be: with men, where two or three are gathered in His name, where the least of His brethren stand in need, where love and charity prevail, wherever there is a good Samaritan or an enemy.

My response is faith. It is the surrender of my life to Christ. Hence it is conversion, *metanoia*; it is also prayer, encounter in Christ with the living God. It is also spiritual renewal, because as Urs von Balthasar has pointed out, renewal is return to the center.

In short, God comes to us through each other and we go to Him through each other. Thus in our response, there are not two movements, one upward, one outward; there is one movement and it involves both God and man at once. This is to say that prayer and community are not disparate activities as they seemed to be in the double movement diagram. Prayer continues to be the search for God, tuning in to Christ. But in this perspective we shall tend to think of Him less apart, in the abstract, in heaven or in the recesses of one's soul, and more as He is one with His brothers and reveals Himself through their humanity and their love. Prayer takes the form of listening, listening to the Other as He is refracted through others. Prayer will continue to include reflective acts in silence; it will celebrate privately and publicly the presence of the Lord in the community. But it can also be mixed up with our interpersonal relationships. Perhaps it would be more heroic if our project were to isolate the Lord and see Him in His transcendent reality, as some of the great saints of the past seemed to do. But who can presume to be called to the heroic? It is significant that President Nixon in his inaugural address emphasized the little virtues, such as lowering our voices and listening to each other. Then he characterized this program in this way:

> I do not offer a life of uninspiring ease.
> I do not call for a life of grim sacrifice.
> I ask you to join in a high adventure—one as rich as
> humanity itself, exciting as the times we live in.

This is the kind of spirituality we are called to practice today. The Holy Spirit has democratized the presence of Christ in our time. Christ speaks to us through each other, across the insights, the aspirations, the problems and preoccupations of man with his fellow man. Today more than ever before, Dostoevsky's words are true: He who desires to see the living God face to face should not seek Him in the empty firmament of his mind, but in human love.

Prayer remains the center of Christian life. But prayer today will take on a different phenomenology. For example, it will more obviously involve the you's in my life. This is because Christ comes to me as I am, namely, not a solitary individual, but a communion, an I-You community.

The response which is prayer remains a personal response to Christ. He will be recognized as a "You" in communion as He was at Emmaus. Thus the word of God addressed to a man is at once a call to be himself, a call to enter into ever deeper communion with his neighbor and with his world, and a call to know and love Christ. It is the call to life, to pass over out of the death of isolation into communion with his fellowmen.

Prayer and communion are so intertwined that they can be separated only by a process of abstraction. The response of faith is the acceptance of God's love. The acceptance can be prayer in the traditional sense, whether of petition—asking to be loved as all our requests of others are—or of contemplation, enjoying what is. But if the response is true and not just mere talk, it is expressed equally well by expressing Christ's and the Father's love to others. My whole life is a response. Through Christ's love both you and I grow together in reconciliation, in community, and in the extension of community to those outside, which we call apostolate. My "Yes" to Christ is immediately and intrinsically a "Yes" to my brothers.

From this we begin to see that renewal of spirit and adaptation of structures are organically interdependent. Structures are the patterns which allow us to communicate with each other, which allow the grace of Christ to influence the community of mankind. They are contingent, indicated or counter-indicated according as they serve or hinder the love of Christ in us. We tend to think of structures only in terms of community life and the apostolate. But they are patterns for prayer as well. Some forms of prayer aid the response of faith, others have become irrelevant, insofar as they do not speak to the religious woman of today.

Prayer and community, i.e. communion, must be *the* values in our life: to appreciate these values anew is to renew ourselves. Prayer structures—"prayers"—are to be promoted which develop our union with Christ, our personal union with the person Christ. There is need for reflective prayer, for the articulation of our surrender to the Lord, for doxology. There is need for prayer together which both celebrates our call together in Christ and gathers us together anew. As for community structures, whatever promotes sound relationships and adult communication, for example, freedom, responsibility, mutual acceptance, mutual support, must be built into the style of religious life of our times. The thesis of this paper is that explicit prayer is the implicit communion with our fellowmen, and the search for communion with each other is implicit prayer. The two supreme values of religious life prosper or weaken together.

The "old spirituality" has been criticized for being one-sidedly theocentric; the "new spirituality" is often accused of being excessively horizontal and secular. The problem of religious renewal is to unite these two approaches, to integrate person, community and God. It does not seem an exaggeration to say that the survival of religious life hangs in the balance. We must reassure ourselves and the young who come to us that religious life is worth it all. It is so, only if it effectively promises union with God and communion with our neighbor. If it does not deliver this genuine friendship with God and each other, it does not deserve to survive.

Let me close with a quotation from John Gardner. According to him institutions are caught today in the crossfire of "uncritical lovers" and "unloving critics." Uncritical lovers "smother their institutions in the embrace of death, loving their rigidities more than their promise, shielding them from life-giving criticism." These are believers in renewal of spirit who refuse to make the necessary changes. The "unloving critics" are the "critics without love," reformers who do not understand and love authentic religious life. They are "skilled in demolition but untutored in the arts by which human institutions are nurtured and strengthened and made to flourish." Let our presence here be our affirmation that we are "critical lovers" of the religious life to which God has called each one of us.